NO
DOUBT
ABOUT

IT

NO
DOUBT
ABOUT
IT

SHERI DEW

BOOKCRAFT

Library of Congress Catalog Card Number: 2001095035

ISBN 1-57345-932-1

Printed in the United States of America   72076-2884
Publishers Printing, Salt Lake City, Utah

10   9   8   7   6   5   4

FOR GRANDMA

Contents

Acknowledgments

I dedicated this book to my grandmother because, even though she died when I was only eleven, her influence on my testimony was penetrating and profound. In the same regard, I express deep gratitude to my parents for teaching me the gospel. I never cease to marvel at the power and responsibility one generation has to influence and teach another.

In like manner, I would hope to have some influence for good on the younger generation in our family. Because this book records the essence of my testimony to this point in my life, I also dedicate it to my favorite young women and young men in heaven and on earth. This book is really for you:

Cory, Lindsay, Megan, Tiffany,
Tanner, Andrew, Breanne,
Aubrey, Amanda, Nicole, Audrey,
Trevor, Emily, Natalie,
Tyson, Matthew,
and Spencer

I HAVE COME TO KNOW
FOR MYSELF

ALTHOUGH THERE ARE MANY THINGS ABOUT THIS LIFE
THAT I DO NOT UNDERSTAND, THERE ARE SOME
TRUTHS ABOUT WHICH I NO LONGER HAVE ANY DOUBT.

A FEW YEARS AGO I was waiting to catch a plane in New York City, and in uncharacteristic fashion I was there enough ahead of time to actually sit down in the airport. As I scanned a newspaper, a commotion caused me to look up, and what I saw made me smile. Walking down the concourse was a large group of missionaries who were talking, laughing, and just generally causing a stir. As they turned *en masse* into my gate and began to present their tickets to the gate agent, it became obvious that we were on the same flight to Salt Lake City. Before we boarded the plane, we had a chance to get acquainted, and I learned that they had each been serving somewhere in eastern Europe—Romania, Ukraine, and Russia among them. These young men and women were bubbling over with the exuberance (and no doubt the anxiety) of returning missionaries and were eager to talk to anyone who would listen about their two-year adventure serving the Lord.

One elder in particular was unforgettable. A young farm boy

from central Utah, he had been serving in Bulgaria. When I asked him about his mission, he said with no small amount of enthusiasm and energy, "*It was great!*"

At that, I pursued a little further: "Elder, I understand that Bulgaria has its challenges. Was your mission difficult?"

"Oh," he responded with passion, "*it was so hard!* You can't imagine how hard it was. My mission must have been the hardest mission in the world!"

I was grinning when I responded: "Well, Elder, if your mission was so difficult, then why was it so great?"

With a flair for the dramatic, he struck a Napoleon-like pose and declared, "Because I did what they sent me to do. And I left Bulgaria better than I found it!"

As we flew back to Salt Lake City, this elder's words kept running through my mind. When it comes time to step across the veil, don't we each hope to be able to give a similar report at the end of our mission here, "I did what I was sent to do. And I tried to leave the people I met and the places I went better than I found them."

President Gordon B. Hinckley expressed a similar sentiment, but with more eloquence: "You are good. But it is not enough just to be good. You must be good for something. You must contribute good to the world. The world must be a better place for your presence. And that good that is in you must be spread to others" (*BYU Speeches of the Year,* 1996).

Playwright Maxwell Anderson put these words into the mouth of the French peasant girl Joan of Arc: "Every woman gives her life for what she believes. Sometimes people believe in little or nothing, nevertheless they give up their lives to that little or nothing. One life is all we have, and we live it as we believe in living it, and then it's gone" (*Joan of Lorraine,* act 2).

I have felt grief. You have felt grief. But I can't imagine pain greater than stepping across the veil and realizing I had not done what I had come here to do—or realizing that I had given up my life to little or nothing, only then to find that it was gone.

We have the magnificent blessing, and the accompanying responsibility, of knowing precisely what we are here for. Our stint in mortality is a "probationary state; a time to prepare to meet God" (Alma 12:24), a time to "repent and serve God" (Alma 42:4), a day "for men [and most assuredly women] to perform their labors" (Alma 34:32), a time to prove whether or not we will do all things that the Lord commands us to do (see Abraham 3:25).

How critical, then, that we be wise and not waste this marvelous but challenging opportunity to prepare and prove ourselves worthy of returning to live with our Father and His Son. Jacob set forth the challenge succinctly: "O be wise; what can I say more?" (Jacob 6:12). And Brigham Young said it this way: "This is a world in which we are to prove ourselves. The lifetime of man is a day of trial, wherein we may prove to God, in our darkness, in our weakness, and where the enemy reigns, that we are our Father's friends" (*Discourses of Brigham Young,* 87). He continued: "You were organized, and brought into being, for the purpose of enduring forever, if you fulfil the measure of your creation, pursue the right path, observe the requirements of the celestial law, and obey the commandments of our God" (*Discourses of Brigham Young,* 87).

So, what have we—as men and women of God, as the Lord's covenant people—come here to do? And amidst all of the challenges and roadblocks, the disappointments and discouragements, the stresses and pressures—how do we do what we have come here to do?

There is much we can learn from Joseph, who was sold into Egypt. Imagine the trauma of being betrayed by his older brothers, separated from his family as a boy, and forced to survive in a completely foreign (and initially hostile) environment. And yet, in spite of these difficult circumstances, Joseph lived with integrity, virtue, and faith.

When he was reunited with his conniving brothers many years later, courtesy of a famine in Canaan that forced them to seek grain in Egypt, an interesting scenario played out. Joseph dispatched his brothers back to Canaan to retrieve their father. Of all the things he could have said to his unreliable brothers as they prepared to depart, his last words of instruction were simply, "See that ye fall not out by the way" (Genesis 45:24).

His words, which are words to live by, remind me of a telegram President George Albert Smith sent to BYU basketball coach Stan Watts and the BYU team prior to their 1951 NIT championship game at Madison Square Garden: "From the top of the Rockies I send my love and blessing. Many thousands share my pride in your record. I have faith in your abilities. Play clean. Play hard. Play fair. Play to win. Return with honor. God bless you." Can't you just picture our Father saying something similar as we prepared to leave our premortal heavenly home and embark upon our mortal experiment? "From the heavens I send with you my love and blessing. Countless of your associates here share pride in your record. I have faith that you can do what you are going to earth to do. Stay clean. Work hard. Be fair with your brothers and sisters. Don't get distracted from doing what you are going there to do. And then return Home, with honor."

President Smith's and Joseph's advice make the reality of the Apostle Paul's final words all the more meaningful: "I have fought a good fight, I have finished my course, I have kept the faith: Henceforth there is laid up for me a crown of righteousness, which the Lord . . . shall give me at that day" (2 Timothy 4:7–8). Again, words to live by—or at least to aim for.

Paul's declaration reminds me of the hymn "Put Your Shoulder to the Wheel," which we sang almost weekly in our little Kansas branch because Grandma played the piano and chose the songs, and she loved the last verse: "Then work and watch and fight and pray with all your might and zeal. Push ev'ry worthy work along; put your shoulder to the wheel" (*Hymns*, no. 252).

All of these words illuminate our goal and our challenge: to keep from falling out by the way on our mortal sojourn. To wage a good fight against the enemy of all righteousness. To finish the custom-made course prepared for each of us. To nourish our faith in Jesus Christ. And then to return Home with honor. In other words, to do what we have come here to do—which will happen only if we work and watch and fight and pray.

Indeed, this process in which we are engaged is glorious but difficult. There are many reasons for this, one of which I learned as a five-foot, ten-inch tomboy who lived and breathed sports. Basketball was my sport of choice, but with a love for sweat socks, the pungent smell of deep-heat ointment, and competition, I played whatever was in season—including fast-pitch softball. During the eighth grade, our small country school had a great fast-pitch softball team, and as the pitcher and captain, I was determined to lead our team to the league championship. Our season went well, and ultimately we found ourselves playing for the title. Everyone turned out for the deciding game, including, of course, my family. The game was tight from the opening pitch, but as we went into the final inning we were ahead 2–1. Then things began to unravel.

First, I walked the lead-off batter. Then the next hitter popped a fly ball to the shortstop, who dropped it. The third batter grounded to the third baseman, who let the ball get past her. The bases were loaded. The next batter hit a line drive right at the first baseman—who ducked. Two runners scored, and my vision of trophies began to evaporate. Then the next hitter whacked the ball deep, and as the left fielder chased it into the corner of the outfield, all of the runners scored.

It perhaps seems odd that I can recall such specific details this many years later. But the episode is engraved in my memory because at that point something happened that I still can't quite explain. From the mound, I began shouting at my teammates. Unfortunately, these weren't the "come-on-you-can-do-it" words of encouragement you would expect and hope to hear from a team captain. This was a good, old-fashioned tongue-lashing in which I basically chewed out the entire infield. This scene had gone on for perhaps a minute when suddenly I realized that I was not alone on the mound.

For there stood Mother, who had seen enough. Taking me by the arm, she escorted me off the field and motioned me into a nearby school bus. Action on the field stopped. The umpire and coaches looked back and forth at each other and then at the school bus where, with her index finger waving in a steady beat,

Mother was issuing an imperative that became indelibly etched in my heart and mind: "*You* are out of control. You have forgotten *who* you are, *where* you are, and what is really important. And if you would *ever* like to play ball again, I suggest that you correct this mistake right now."

Suddenly horrified at the realization of what I had done, and humbled by Mother's chastening, I walked sheepishly off the bus. With hundreds of pairs of eyes watching me, I walked to the umpire and apologized. Then to my coach and apologized. Then to my teammates and apologized. And then back to the mound to play out the final inning.

We lost the game.

But worse, I lost the opportunity to accept defeat graciously, to support my teammates in a time of disappointment, to lose with honor and self-respect.

Mother was right. I had been out of control. I had forgotten who I was and what standard of behavior was expected of me; where I was and what was appropriate on a ball diamond and during a game; and what was important—which was not only to play well but to behave well.

It seems to be easy here in mortality to do what I did—to lose sight of who we are and what we're here for, and as a result to become distracted from what is really important. If we don't have a clear sense of our identity and purpose, we are much more vulnerable to Lucifer. He of course knows this and accordingly attempts to blur our vision. He lies. He shades and obliterates truth. He makes evil look good and good look unenlightened and unsophisticated. Make no mistake about it: Lucifer will do *anything* to derail, disappoint, dishearten, discourage, and deceive us—and particularly those who have made and are seeking to keep sacred covenants. His motives are entirely self-centered, selfish, destructive, and evil.

From the adversary's point of view, *we are dangerous.* Righteous women and righteous men dedicated to the Lord and united in the cause of goodness threaten Satan's work. Of course he would target and attempt to deceive us, women who have a clear understanding of who we are. *For we are not ordinary women.*

We know that we are beloved spirit daughters of heavenly parents, and that our lives have meaning, purpose, and direction, as the Relief Society Declaration asserts (see *Ensign,* November 1999, 92–93). We are women who seek to hear the voice of the Lord. We are women dedicated to strengthening our marriages, families, and homes; women whose covenants and influence span generations; women who are not easily deceived; women of faith, virtue, vision, and charity—not to mention integrity and purity. We are women who understand that to qualify for eternal life, we must deal with a full range of difficulty and disappointment here. We are free to choose how we live, where we spend our temporal, emotional, and spiritual resources, and to what and whom we devote ourselves.

My first seminary teacher, who remained a dear friend and example throughout his life, seized every opportunity to teach the gospel—including during a hospital stay where he learned that his nurse was taking the missionary discussions. One evening they talked for several hours about the plan of salvation. At the conclusion of their talk, she summed up their conversation by saying, "Satan sure doesn't end up with much, does he?"

No, Satan won't end up with much, and neither will those who are duped into following him. Hence our challenge to walk the straight and narrow path until the end of our probation. To not fall out by the way. To do what we have come here to do. And to leave the people we meet and the places we visit better than we found them.

Our ability to successfully negotiate this spiritual mine field called mortality improves dramatically if we are clear about who we are and what is important. And what is important is eternal life. Said President Spencer W. Kimball, "Since immortality and eternal life constitute the sole purpose of life, all other interests and activities are but incidental thereto" (*The Miracle of Forgiveness,* 2).

Does that mean there should be no ballgames or barbecues or ballets? Of course not. But it does mean that we must be riveted on our goal. Anything that takes us closer to exaltation is worth our time and energy. Anything that doesn't is a distraction. Brigham Young taught: "To be sealed up to the day of redemption and have the promise of eternal lives, is the greatest gift of all. The people do not fully understand these things and have them not in full vision before their minds, if they did I will tell you, plainly and in honesty, that there is not a trial which the Saints are called to pass through that they would not realize and acknowledge to be their greatest blessing" (*Journal of Discourses,* 2:301).

Of course our faith will be tried. Of course we will have tests of our will, of our endurance, of our desires, and of our determination and conviction. Lorenzo Snow said: "The Lord . . . will try us until He knows what He can do with us. He tried His Son Jesus. Thousands of years before he came upon the earth the Father had watched His course and knew that He could depend upon Him when the salvation of worlds should be at stake. . . .

He will . . . continue to try us, in order that He may place us in the highest positions in life and put upon us the most sacred responsibilities" (*Millennial Star,* 24 August 1899, 532).

It is in moments of disappointment, heartache, and loneliness that we often make the decisions that forge our faith, mold our character, and fortify our convictions about the only source of strength and solace that satisfies. And that is Jesus Christ. How do we know if we are honest, unless our honesty is put to the test? How do we know if we are filled with virtue, unless there are opportunities to choose a nonvirtuous path that we then resist? How do we know if we can bear up under challenge and trial, unless we have challenge and trial? And how can we expect to feel and taste the pure sweetness of the gospel of Jesus Christ, meaning specifically the power and peace of the atonement of Jesus Christ, unless there are times in our lives when we desperately need and seek that peace and power?

Weekly we partake of the sacrament to renew our covenant to "always remember" the Lord (Moroni 4:3; 5:2). Imagine how our perspective and behavior would be affected if we truly always remembered Him, because remembering the Lord and remembering who we are seem to be inseparably connected.

In the movie *The Lion King,* the lion cub Simba forsakes his heritage and turns to riotous living after the death of his father, Mufasa. But when that lifestyle fails to satisfy his inner self, Simba turns to the heavens in a moment of desperation. His father responds by appearing to him, and after listening to Simba's attempts to justify his behavior, Mufasa delivers profound parting words: "You have forgotten who you are, because you have forgotten me. You have become less than who you are."

Like the lion cub Simba, we live in a complex world, one filled with choices and opportunities and also with confusion and conflicting voices. It is a world that increasingly doesn't know God and certainly doesn't know how (or even believe it is possible) to communicate with God; a world where conspiring and confused men and women call evil good and good evil; a world where many have lost sight of values and don't even believe a code of ethics is realistic anymore. In our world there are ongoing debates on the national and international stage about topics that would have seemed ludicrous a decade or two ago, topics such as what is and is not moral, what is and is not honest—and whether or not morality or integrity even matter. Our elected officials disappoint and even lie to us, and a proliferation of loud and conflicting voices are bent on getting our money, our support, our vote, and even our virtue. Many, perhaps most, of these voices are motivated largely by self-interest and have no concern about what is best for us or about what is right or wrong.

No wonder Elder Neal A. Maxwell said that "though we have rightly applauded our ancestors for their spiritual achievement . . . those of us who prevail today will have done no small thing. The special spirits who have been reserved to live in this time of challenges and who overcome will one day be praised for their stamina by those who pulled handcarts" (*Notwithstanding My Weakness*, 18).

So, what are we do to? Life is filled with moments of joy, but life is also hard. It is an unmistakable privilege to be here in mortality, but the burden we carry is weighty, relentless, and laden with importance. So I repeat two questions posed earlier: What have we come here to do? And how will we do it?

There are many things about mortality that I do not yet—and may never in this life—understand. But there are some truths about which I no longer have any doubt, truths that I believe are keys to successfully negotiating mortality.

With Alma, I say that there are some things I have come to know of myself (see Alma 5:46): that Jesus is the Christ, that His gospel has been restored, and that living the gospel is the only way to find happiness here or hereafter.

I know that the light of Jesus Christ is stronger than any kind of darkness we face here; that we each have purpose; that understanding who we are and who we have always been is central to our mortal success and eternal progression; that the family and the Church family are where we can find safety and refuge; that while life is a test, we have magnificent spiritual privileges as members of the Church to help us meet that test.

I know that, as difficult a challenge as mortality is, we are not alone here, because among our privileges as covenanted members of the Church are the gift of the Holy Ghost, the power of the priesthood, ordinances that bind us to each other and to the Lord, and a living prophet. I know that as we let the world go and become consecrated followers of Jesus Christ, we will be better able to fill our foreordained missions here in helping build the kingdom of God. And I know that every one of us is vital to building that kingdom.

These are some of the truths upon which I have focused this book.

We have so much more than we sometimes realize. I thought about this when we, as a Relief Society general presidency, were invited to attend a luncheon honoring representatives of a national Christian organization. I was quite taken with one of the guests, a woman who was herself a minister, whose husband was a minister, and whose parents on both sides of the family were ministers. She had been raised to believe in Jesus Christ. She had been to divinity school, was a judicious student of the Bible, and had devoted her life to teaching the gospel as she knew it. I liked this woman instantly. She was obviously a great mother and a devoted wife. I found myself wishing I could live next door to her.

Toward the end of our luncheon, she commented on the kindness of everyone at Church headquarters and how much she had enjoyed her trip to Salt Lake City. And then she said something I will never forget: "I want you to know that I believe in God. I don't really know how He talks to us, but I know that He does."

It was everything I could do to not leap to my feet and exclaim, "*We know!* We know how the Lord talks to us. May we tell you?" I felt bad for this good woman, who despite all of her study didn't begin to comprehend the scope of the fulness of the gospel of Jesus Christ. She didn't have the privilege of a living prophet, or the constant companionship of the Holy Ghost, or access to priesthood power. She had a sense that God watches over us and communicates with us, but she didn't know how.

As you read this book, I invite you to consider anew what you know and what you have; what you are here for and where you are going; and how you are going to do what you have come here to do. I invite you to go before the Lord and ask the Spirit to talk to you through these pages, so that you can learn and hear what *you* need to learn and hear. And I pray that through this exercise, you will solidify in your heart and in your mind those things about which you, too, have absolutely no doubt.

CHAPTER 1

THE LIGHT IS STRONGER THAN THE DARK

GOD IS OUR FATHER, JESUS IS THE CHRIST, AND, AS A
PROPHET HAS SAID, OUR GREATEST NEED IS TO
INCREASE OUR FAITH. THUS, OUR CONNECTION WITH
THE DIVINE DEPENDS ALMOST ENTIRELY UPON US.

SOME YEARS AGO on a trip to Dallas, Texas, I took in an evening basketball game with friends. When we emerged from the arena, we found the area socked in with a dense, almost suffocating kind of fog. With little choice but to try to find our way home, we joined the hundreds of other cars inching their way down the freeway. The fog was so thick and heavy that we couldn't see the ornament on the front of the hood, let alone the lines on the side of the road. It felt as though we were driving straight into a clam-chowder-like abyss. It was unnerving and tedious—enough so that my friends' young son began to get restless and climb from seat to seat.

But then without warning something through the front windshield caught his attention, and he quieted down. Pointing toward the two thin streams of light coming from the headlights, which were cutting narrow channels in the dense fog before dissipating into the dark of night, he said to his father, "Look, Dad, the light is pushing away the dark. How does it do that, Dad?" Before his father could respond, the boy interrupted: "Oh, I know. The light is stronger than the dark, isn't it, Dad?"

That was nearly two decades ago. But I can still picture looking at this boy's mother, who had also been struck by her son's comment, and then sitting back to ponder the significance of the truth he had unwittingly articulated.

The light *is* stronger than the dark, and Jesus Christ is the Ultimate Light. During His earthly ministry the Savior proclaimed, "I am the light of the world: he that followeth me shall not walk in darkness, but shall have the light of life" (John 8:12). And to Joseph Smith and Oliver Cowdery He explained, "I am the light which shineth in darkness, and the darkness comprehendeth it not" (D&C 6:21). It is as Abinadi taught the unrepentant Nephites, "He is the light and the life of the world; yea, a light that is endless, *that can never be darkened*" (Mosiah 16:9; emphasis added).

There are many kinds of darkness that can come into our lives. Loneliness, discouragement, and disappointment can cause us to feel a kind of darkness. Betrayal and pain can do likewise. When we make foolish mistakes or succumb to sin, we can expect to feel varying degrees of darkness, depending on our motive and intent as well as on the light and knowledge we have enjoyed previously. But there is one source of Light that pushes away all darkness, as the Lord taught the Prophet Joseph through revelation: "That which is of God is light; and he that receiveth light, and continueth in God, receiveth more light; and that light groweth brighter and brighter until the perfect day. . . . And I say it that you may know the truth, that you may chase darkness from among you" (D&C 50:24–25).

That little boy fascinated with the fog taught a profound truth: The light *is* stronger than the dark. The power of Jesus Christ is stronger than anything we can expect to face in this world, including the power of Satan. The Savior's light is greater than any heartache or loneliness, more powerful than any kind of pain, stronger than any weakness or temptation.

No wonder, then, that faith is the first principle of the gospel of Jesus Christ, for it is our willingness and ability to believe in Jesus Christ—to believe that He is who He has said He is, and that He will do for us what He has said He will do—that activates the power of the Atonement in our lives.

A ten-year-old girl caught the essence of this. After watching a science fiction series on television, she said in the family prayer, "Please bless the earth that it will be protected by a force field." In essence, that is what the Lord has pledged—that if we come unto Him, have faith in Him, and seek after Him, He will push the darkness of mortality away from us with His power. "If your eye be single to my glory," He said, "your whole bodies shall be filled with light, and there shall be no darkness in you; and that body which is filled with light comprehendeth all things" (D&C 88:67).

How crucial it is for each of us to understand the source and power of the Ultimate Light, the Light that can push away the various kinds of darkness of mortality, the Light that will illuminate the path that leads back Home.

It was when I was a young BYU student that I learned a little something about staying on course, or on the right path, when heading home. One Christmas Eve morning my younger brother and I left to drive from Provo, Utah, to our parents' home in Kansas. Early in our journey we learned via radio reports that our path was taking us directly into a huge snowstorm, so we pulled out a map, identified a detour that we thought would skirt the edge of the storm, and headed into parts unknown. Our creative navigating proved dangerous, for our new route was totally unfamiliar, and we still ran right into the blizzard. To make matters worse, late that night as we were creeping along in blinding snow on an obscure highway in the middle of nowhere, our old Ford quit. We were stranded. And we had absolutely no idea where we were.

Eventually, and fortunately, we caught a ride to the nearest town, where we found that we were still hours from home and marooned in a little wide spot in the road called Last Chance, Colorado. At that point there was only one thing to do. We called home for help. In the middle of the night our father left to come and rescue us. He found the car we had abandoned at the side of a deserted, two-lane country highway. More importantly, he found us. By the next afternoon we were all safely home.

I'll never forget Christmas Eve in Last Chance, where we were immobilized by a problem largely of our own making that we were unequipped to solve. That day our father did for us what we could not do for ourselves. He rescued us and helped us resume our journey home.

Now, each one of us is on the path toward our eternal home. And for various reasons and at varying times we all need rescue— rescue from loneliness and heartache, from despair and disillusionment, from the consequences of innocent mistakes and blatant sin.

Where do we turn for help? Toward the Light. For "in the gift of his Son hath God prepared a more excellent way" (Ether 12:11). The Savior isn't our last chance; He is our only chance. Our only chance to overcome self-doubt and catch a vision of who we may become. Our only chance to repent and have our sins washed clean. Our only chance to purify our hearts, subdue our weaknesses, and avoid the adversary. Our only chance to obtain redemption and exaltation. Our only chance to find peace and happiness in this life and eternal life in the world to come.

Left to his own devices, the natural man almost inevitably succumbs to Satan (see Mosiah 3:19), who ensnares his prey and then fails to support them once he has lured them from the straight and narrow path. But the Savior will guide those who follow Him all the way home. Lehi's family endured an intense wilderness experience designed to teach, test, and sanctify them. Likewise, the path from our former home to eternal life runs right through this earthly wilderness, where we may expect similar challenges and difficulties. But in our journey we are not alone, for the Lord's promise to Nephi is the same to us: "I will prepare the way before you . . . [and] inasmuch as ye shall keep my commandments ye shall be led towards the promised land. . . . After ye have arrived . . . ye shall know that . . . the Lord, did deliver you" (1 Nephi 17:13–14). Remember what the Lord has pledged to all who diligently seek after Him: "I will be a light unto them forever, that hear my words" (2 Nephi 10:14).

The Lord knows the way because *He is the way*. He is our only chance for successfully negotiating mortality. His Atonement makes available all of the power, peace, light, and strength that we need to deal with life's challenges—those ranging from our own mistakes and sins to trials over which we have no control but still feel pain.

The Lord has promised to heal our broken hearts and "to set at liberty them that are bruised" (Luke 4:18); to give power to the faint, to heal the wounded soul, and to turn our weakness into strength (see Isaiah 40:29; Jacob 2:8; Ether 12:27); to take upon Him our pains and sicknesses, to blot out our transgressions if we repent, and to loose the bands of death (see Alma 7:11–13). He has promised that if we will build our lives upon His rock, the devil will have no power over us (see Helaman 5:12). And He has vowed that He will never leave us or forsake us (see Hebrews 13:5). There is simply no mortal equivalent, not in terms of commitment, power, or love. He is our only chance. He is the Ultimate Light.

Our responsibility, then, is to learn to draw upon the power of the Atonement. Otherwise we walk through mortality relying solely on our own strength. And to do that is to invite the frustration of failure and to refuse the most resplendent gift in time or eternity. My brother and I would have been foolish to not seek or accept our father's help when we were stranded. Likewise, the Lord is our advocate, and He "knoweth the weakness of man and how to succor them who are tempted" (D&C 62:1). In other words, He knows how to succor *all* of us. But we must activate the power of the Atonement in our lives. We do this by first believing in Him, by repenting, by obeying His commandments, by partaking of sacred ordinances and keeping covenants, and by seeking after Him in fasting and prayer, in the scriptures, and in the temple.

All of this requires our faith in the Lord. President Gordon B.

Hinckley has said that "if there is any one thing you and I need . . . it is faith" (*Teachings of Gordon B. Hinckley,* 186). To have faith in Christ is to believe in Him, follow Him, and rely on Him. And it is to be blessed with the peace of conscience and mind that the Apostle Paul spoke of when he said, "I can do all things through Christ which strengtheneth me" (Philippians 4:13).

During the 1950s, Elder Ezra Taft Benson served for eight years as Secretary of Agriculture under U.S. President Dwight D. Eisenhower. In addition to his high-pressure Cabinet assignment, which often found him in the midst of controversy spawned by his agricultural policies, he was a member of the Quorum of the Twelve Apostles, and as such represented the Church in every setting in which he found himself. On top of that, he was a husband and a father of six. A Church member who worked in the Department of Agriculture asked Elder Benson one day how he did it—how he managed to handle the workload, the pressure, and the relentless criticism aired regularly on the nightly news, and to do so while retaining the dignity and deportment of his Church calling. He replied in words to this effect, "I work as hard as I can, and I try my best to be obedient so that the Lord knows I am mindful of Him. Then I have the faith that He will make up the difference between what I am able to do, and what I am not able to do. And He does." That is simple but pure faith.

I recall a meeting we had, as a Relief Society general presidency, with two journalists from a nation in eastern Europe who were intrigued about service that had been performed by our sisters in their country. We explained that from its earliest days this grand organization of righteous women had sought not only to "relieve the poor but to save souls" (Relief Society Minutebook,

9 June 1842). When these European journalists asked if we helped women with their "emotional problems," explaining that many in their country were discouraged, we responded that in Relief Society we study the doctrines of the gospel, and the gospel teaches us how to be happy even when life is hard. One of the reporters was incredulous: "Is it possible?" she asked. "Is it possible to be happy when life is hard?" Her question tugged at me. I knew that, for her, life was an exercise in enduring drudgery, and that she did not know where to turn for peace.

Is it possible to be happy when life is hard? Can we feel peace amid uncertainty, or hope in the midst of cynicism? Is it possible to change, to shake off old habits and become new again? Is it possible to live with integrity and purity in a world that no longer values the virtues that distinguish the followers of Christ?

Yes. The answer is an unqualified *yes* because of Jesus Christ, whose Atonement and Light ensure that we need not bear the burdens or the darkness of mortality alone. There is nothing this confused world needs more, nothing that inspires a greater sense of well-being, nothing that has greater power to strengthen families than the gospel of Jesus Christ. Elder Howard W. Hunter said that "whatever Jesus lays his hands upon lives. If Jesus lays his hands upon a marriage, it lives. If he is allowed to lay his hands on the family, *it lives*" (In Conference Report, October 1979, 93; emphasis added). The Savior will do for each of us what He has promised to do—if we will have faith in Him and receive His gift.

Through the years I, like you, have experienced pressures and disappointments that would have crushed me had I not been able to draw on a source of wisdom and strength far greater than my own. Jesus Christ, the source of ultimate power and light, has never forgotten or forsaken me, and over time I have come to know for myself that He is the Christ, the Redeemer of us all, and that this is His Church. With Ammon I say, "Who can glory too much in the Lord? Yea, who can say too much of his great power, and of his mercy . . . ? Behold, . . . I cannot say the smallest part which I feel" (Alma 26:16). During this day when Lucifer is working overtime to jeopardize our journey home and to separate us from the Savior's atoning power and light, the only answer for any of us is Jesus Christ.

May we therefore recommit to seek after this Jesus, of whom the prophets have testified. May we yoke ourselves to Him, draw liberally upon the matchless power of His Atonement, and rise up as sons and daughters of God and shake off the world. To "those who will have him to be their God" (1 Nephi 17:40), the Lord has extended a magnificent promise: "I will go before your face. I will be on your right hand and on your left, and my Spirit shall be in your hearts, and mine angels round about you, to bear you up" (D&C 84:88). Jesus Christ is not our last chance, He is our only chance. He will show us the way because He *is* the way, and He lights the way.

CHAPTER 2

THE MIRACLE
OF PARLEY STREET

WHEN WE COME TO KNOW FOR OURSELVES
THAT JESUS IS THE CHRIST,
OUR LIVES CAN NEVER BE THE SAME AGAIN.

I WAS RAISED ON A FARM in Kansas where we lived next door to my Grandma Dew, and I was her shadow. We went everywhere together—to the bank, the doctor, the Early Bird Garden Club, and an endless procession of Church meetings. When it came to the gospel, Grandma was zealous. She would talk about the gospel anytime, anywhere, and with anyone—including her eldest granddaughter. During most of my growing-up years, she served as a family history specialist for our mission, which then took in four states, and when she traveled she often took me with her. So we went to a lot of meetings together.

I'll never forget an interchange she and I had one night as we drove home from yet another long meeting. It began when I blurted out a question that flashed through my eight-year-old mind: "Grandma, what if the gospel isn't true and we've been going to all of these meetings for nothing?"

"Sheri, you don't need to worry about that," she answered, "because the gospel is true. I am sure of it."

I didn't understand how she could be so sure, and so I challenged her: "But how can you know for sure?"

Several seconds passed before she said slowly, "I know for sure that the gospel is true because the Holy Ghost has told me that Jesus Christ is our Savior and that this is His Church."

"But Grandma," I protested, "there is no way you can know *for absolute sure.*"

There was a pause, and then she added something I will never forget: "Sheri, I do know. The Lord has told me. And He'll tell you too. And when He does, your life can never be the same again."

I still vividly remember what happened next. A sensation unlike any I had ever experienced charged through my body, and then I began to cry. Though I didn't understand the reason for my outburst, I'm sure Grandma realized exactly what was happening. The Spirit was bearing witness to me that what she had said was true.

Now, nearly four decades later, I am grateful that during the intervening years I have come to know for myself that Jesus is the Christ, our Savior and our Redeemer, and that once you have that knowledge your life can never be the same again.

Prophets, ancient and modern, have urged us to come unto Christ (see Ether 12:41; Moroni 10:32). President Gordon B. Hinckley declared that "[Jesus Christ] is the pivotal figure of our theology and our faith. Every Latter-day Saint has the responsibility to know . . . with a certainty beyond doubt that Jesus is the resurrected, living Son of the living God" (*Ensign*, May 1983, 80).

The admonition to "come unto Christ" is the hub around which everything in The Church of Jesus Christ of Latter-day

Saints revolves—and for good reason. The verb *come* implies action on our part. In the familiar New Testament passage about the hereafter in which many plead their case with the Lord by listing all of their good deeds, Christ responds, "I never knew you" (Matthew 7:23). Joseph Smith's inspired translation of that same passage, however, notes a profound distinction: "[You] never knew *me*" (JST, Matthew 7:33; emphasis added). That places responsibility for coming unto the Savior squarely upon our shoulders.

Jesus Christ Himself has promised, "Draw near unto me and I will draw near unto you; seek me diligently and ye shall find me; ask, and ye shall receive; knock, and it shall be opened unto you" (D&C 88:63). There are no disclaimers or exceptions in His invitation. *We* are the ones who determine whether or not we will come unto Him. The drawing near, seeking, asking, and knocking are up to us. And the more we know about the Lord—meaning the more we experience His mercy, devotion, and willingness to guide us even when we may not feel worthy of His direction—the more confident we become that He will respond to our petitions.

A single mother of six who had been divorced for more than ten years wrote this in a letter to Church headquarters: "A month before my divorce was final, I was in an accident where I broke ten bones in my foot. Within the next four years, I had more than fourteen surgeries and continued raising my children as well as keeping my teaching certificate current. I found so much peace through my obedience in daily scripture study and prayer with my children, as well as my own individual study. I also received great inner strength through my regular attendance at the temple. I can testify that when we do what the Lord has asked us to do, He will bless us. I am so thankful for my testimony and to know that I am a child of God and that He will not give us more than we can bear."

As this sister expressed, when we increase our interaction with the Lord, we learn for ourselves that He will never betray us, never forget us or leave us alone, never turn away, never change His criteria for our coming unto Him. His attention is riveted on us, His brothers and sisters.

There are many ways to draw near, seek, ask, and knock. If, for example, our prayers offered to Heavenly Father in the name of Christ have become a little casual, could we not recommit ourselves to meaningful prayer, offered in unrushed solitude and with a repentant heart? If we have not yet come to appreciate the peace and the power of temple worship, could we partake of the ordinances of the house of the Lord as often as our circumstances allow, pleading with the Lord to help us understand how what we are learning can strengthen, protect, guide, and help us solve our daily problems? If we have not yet found that ongoing immersion in the scriptures increases our sensitivity to the Spirit, could we consider incorporating the word of God into our lives more consistently and regularly, and with greater intent? There is no better time to begin than today.

These efforts and many others increase our connection with Jesus Christ. As our testimony of Him expands and matures, we begin to care more about life forever than life today, we begin to care less about the enticements of the world and more about the possibility of life everlasting and never-ending happiness. And we have no desire but to do what He needs us to do and to live as He has asked us to live. President Ezra Taft Benson taught that "when you choose to follow Christ, you choose to be changed" (*Ensign*, November 1985, 5). It is a lot like what Grandma told me: "When you have a testimony of Jesus Christ, your life can never be the same again."

I remember with delight a vacation I took to the exquisite Oregon coast. Because I was there over a weekend, I had the chance to visit a ward there, and at the conclusion of sacrament meeting I was a little surprised when a woman approached me and asked, "Are you the woman I think you are?" She thought she recognized me, and her question referred to my identity, but it is a question that has haunted me ever since. *Am* I the woman I think I am, the woman I want to be? More importantly, am I the woman the Savior needs me to be?

There is a connection between my Oregon friend's question and the lesson I learned from Grandma, for there is a direct relationship between how we see ourselves and how we feel about Jesus Christ. We cannot increase our devotion to the Savior without also obtaining a greater sense of purpose, identity, and conviction.

When I think of having a sense of purpose, I always think of the early members of the Church. I love Nauvoo. The feelings and thoughts I have there are unique. I love to walk the roads, to gaze upon the temple lot that now houses a magnificent temple, to imagine Joseph and Brigham and Emma and Eliza and Heber and so many others coming and going, preaching and prophesying, and building the small but growing kingdom of God. But there is one place in Nauvoo that, for me, evokes unusual emotion.

Every time I visit the City of Joseph, I walk to the end of Parley Street, where the Saints lined up their wagons as they prepared once again to leave their homes and evacuate the city. There I try to imagine how our pioneer sisters must have felt as they loaded what little they could into their wagons, glanced a final time at the nearly completed temple on the hill and at their homes, and then followed their faith into the wilderness. It's a miracle, really—a miracle wrought by faith.

I always weep on Parley Street because I can't help but wonder, Would I have loaded that wagon? Would my testimony of a modern-day prophet and my faith in Jesus Christ have been strong enough that I would have given up everything and gone anywhere?

I had the same kind of reaction at Albert Dock in Liverpool, England—the dock from which thousands of British converts departed the British Isles in the 1840s and 1850s to join the Saints in the West. Once again, as I walked across the rough-hewn cobblestones that Brigham and Heber and Parley trod when they arrived in England to spread the gospel, I wondered: Would I have done it? Would I have boarded a small ship, sailed out into the Irish Sea, crossed the Atlantic, and headed for parts unknown? Would my testimony of a modern-day prophet and my faith in Jesus Christ have been strong enough that I would have given up everything—even my native land—and gone anywhere?

Perhaps few of us today will be called upon to suffer deprivation because of what we believe. Perhaps few will be required to sacrifice our homes or the soil where we have grown gardens and raised our families. But we have been called to live in a time when the chasm between the philosophies of men and the teachings of the Master gapes wider than ever. We have been required to face the world at its worst, and to stand true and faithful in spite of the temptations to the contrary.

Each day we stand at the end of our own Parley Street. Each day we stand on our own pier at Albert Dock. Each day we have the privilege of choosing whom we will follow. Each day we have opportunities to bolster and strengthen and exercise our faith. The Lord needed the strength of the women of this Church as the seeds of the Restoration were planted and nourished. And He needs us today. He needs us to speak up for what is right, even when doing so is unpopular. He needs us to develop the spiritual maturity to hear the voice of the Lord and detect the deceptions of the adversary. He needs us to be everything we can be, to "arise and shine forth, that [our] light may be a standard for the nations" (D&C 115:5).

Are we the women we think we are? Are we the women the Lord needs us to be? Have we received a testimony of Jesus Christ and His gospel such that our lives can simply never be the same again?

I will not soon forget a brief conversation I had with President Hinckley during which, in response to a question he raised about my calling to serve in the general presidency of the Relief Society, I said, "I love being with the women of the Church. They are so good." Instantly he corrected me: "No, Sheri. They aren't good. They are great!"

I take prophets at their word. And our prophet believes in us. He believes in our spiritual strength and our resilience, in our faith as well as our faithfulness. Regardless of your marital status, your age, or the language you speak, you are a beloved spirit daughter of Heavenly Father who is destined to play a critical part in the onward movement of the gospel kingdom. Eliza R. Snow proclaimed that "it is the duty of each one of us to be a holy woman. . . . There is no sister so isolated, and her sphere so narrow but what she can do a great deal towards establishing the Kingdom of God upon the earth" (*Woman's Exponent,* 15 September 1873, 62).

Remember Grandma? She lived a simple life in an obscure corner of the vineyard. Her face never graced a magazine cover. She never obtained riches or became famous by the world's standards. At this point, there are only a handful of people still living who even remember her.

But I remember her. Though she died when I was just eleven, I was profoundly influenced by this one faithful woman. Like Grandma, each of us is vital to the Lord's cause and each of us is in a position to have profound, everlasting influence. How much good might we do if, without delay, we rededicated ourselves to Him who is our Redeemer and our Rescuer? How much righteous influence might we have if we joined the Young Women in their pledge to "stand as witnesses of God at all times and in all things, and in all places" (Mosiah 18:9)?

Happily, we are all in this together. But the question remains: Are we the women the Lord needs us to be? Might we not commit to do just a little better than we have been doing, and in the process marshal our forces to lead the women of the world in all that is Godlike and ennobling?

My grandma was right. When we come to know that Jesus is the Christ, our lives can never be the same again. With Grandma, I know that the Savior is the one source of strength and comfort and light that we can count on. He came to succor us in our infirmities and to heal our broken hearts. As Mormon told his son Moroni, after describing the depraved state into which the Nephite nation had fallen, "Be faithful in Christ; and may not the things which I have written grieve thee, to weigh thee down . . . but may Christ lift thee up" (Moroni 9:25). Indeed, the Savior is eager to light our path and to lift us up—if we will come unto Him.

Moroni's benedictory testimony charts our course: "Awake, and arise from the dust, O Jerusalem; yea, and put on thy beautiful garments, O daughter of Zion. . . . Yea, come unto Christ, and be perfected in him, and deny yourselves of all ungodliness; and if ye shall deny yourselves of all ungodliness, and love God with all your might, mind and strength, then is his grace sufficient for you, that by his grace ye may be perfect in Christ" (Moroni 10:31–32).

Everything the Savior did in the Garden of Gethsemane and on the cross at Calvary was for us. Other than fulfilling the obligation He had made to His Father, there was nothing in it for Him personally. He was already the God of the Old Testament, the Creator of the heavens and the earth. God gave us the sacrifice of His Son, and His Son gave us His life. That is how important we are to our Father and to His Only Begotten Son, our Elder Brother.

Our challenge, then, is to strengthen our resolve to follow our Savior and to be the women that He needs us to be.

CHAPTER 3

REMEMBERING WHO YOU ARE . . . AND WHO YOU HAVE ALWAYS BEEN

WHEN WE COME TO UNDERSTAND NOT ONLY WHO WE
ARE BUT WHO WE HAVE ALWAYS BEEN—
AND THEREFORE WHO WE MAY BECOME—
THE CHOICE BETWEEN FOLLOWING CHRIST OR
EMBRACING THE WORLD IS REALLY NO CHOICE AT ALL.

RECENTLY MY SIXTEEN-YEAR-OLD NIECE Megan and two of her friends came for a sleepover. As we talked that evening, I asked, "What do you think someone my age doesn't understand about being your age?" Were they ever eager to talk—about peers and pressure and so on. At one point, one of them asked me what it had been like growing up on a farm in the *olden days.* (Of course, I guess that was no worse than a returned missionary who recently said, "Sister Dew, if I were just *forty years older* I'd marry you!") Anyway, I told the girls that in the "olden days" I had been painfully shy and had always felt awkward, inferior, and that I just didn't measure up.

"How did you get over feeling that way?" Megan asked. A pat answer was on the tip of my tongue when I stopped, sensing that these terrific young women were ready for and deserved to hear more. So I told them that the answer had two parts: that while the requirements of my profession had helped ease some of my inherent shyness, the real reason was a spiritual one. It wasn't until I began to understand how the *Lord* felt about me that my feelings about myself began to change. Their questions then came in a flurry: How did I *know* how the Lord felt? And how could *they* know how He felt about *them?* For hours, scriptures in hand, we talked about learning how to hear the voice of the Spirit. We discussed how eager the Lord is to unveil the knowledge stored safely inside our spirits about who we are and what our mission is. And we talked about the life-changing difference it makes when we know.

I have no doubt about what I told those girls that evening. Truly, there is nothing more vital to our success and our happiness here in mortality than learning to hear the voice of the Spirit, for it is the Spirit who reveals to us our identity—which isn't just who we are, but *who we have always been.* And when we know, our lives take on a purpose so stunning that we are changed forever.

As a people we talk and sing constantly about being sons and daughters of God. Three-year-olds know the words to "I Am a Child of God." As our youth walk out the door, we call behind them, "Remember who you are!" The second Young Women's value is *divine nature.* The Proclamation on the Family declares that we each have "a divine nature and destiny." And the first words in the Relief Society Declaration are "We are beloved spirit daughters of God, and our lives have meaning, purpose, and direc- tion." And yet, with all our talk, do we really believe? Do we really understand? Has this transcendent doctrine about who we are, meaning who we have always been and therefore who we may become, penetrated our hearts?

Our spirits long for us to remember the truth about who we are, because the way we see ourselves, or our sense of identity, affects *everything* we do. It affects the way we behave, the way we respond to uncertainty, the way we see others, the way we handle pressure and disappointment, the way we feel about ourselves, and the way we make choices. In short, it determines how we live our lives. So, the question we might all do well to ponder is not only who we are, but who we have always been.

Lorenzo Snow taught that "Jesus was a god before he came into the world and yet his knowledge was taken from him. He did not know his former greatness, neither do we know what greatness we had attained to before we came here" (Office Journal of Lorenzo Snow, 8 October 1900, 181–82). But President Snow also taught that during the Savior's life "it was revealed unto Him who He was, and for what purpose He was in the world. The glory and power He possessed *before* He came into the world was made known unto Him" (in Conference Report, April 1901, 3; emphasis added). Just as the Savior came to understand exactly who He was, so may we.

Unlocking this knowledge would be easier if we could remember what happened in the premortal world. But we can't. We can't remember the glory of our former home—which is just as well, for "we would pine for it," said President George Q. Cannon, who served as a counselor to four presidents of the Church (*Gospel Truth*, 8). We have forgotten the language we spoke there and our dear companions with whom we associated. We can't remember how we lived there or in what configurations.

We cannot recall the "first lessons [we learned] in the world of spirits" (D&C 138:56) or the identities of our heavenly tutors and trainers who taught us perfectly. We can't remember what promises we made to ourselves, to others, and to the Lord. Nor can we remember our place in the Lord's heavenly kingdom or the spiritual maturity we achieved there. Thus, at times, we may feel more like "strangers and foreigners" than "fellowcitizens with the saints" (Ephesians 2:19).

There are, however, some remarkable things we *do* know. We know that *we were there,* in the heavenly councils before the foundations of this earth were laid. Said President Joseph F. Smith, "We were there; we were interested, and we took a part in this great preparation. We were unquestionably present in those councils . . . when Satan offered himself as a savior of the world if he could but receive the honor and glory of the Father for doing it. . . . We were, no doubt, there, and took part in all those scenes, we were vitally concerned in the carrying out of these great plans and purposes, we understood them, and it was for our sakes they were decreed, and are to be consummated" (*Gospel Doctrine,* 93–94).

We were there when our Father presented His plan, and we saw the Savior chosen and appointed—and, as the Prophet Joseph taught, we "sanctioned it" (*Teachings,* 181). *We were there* among the heavenly host who sang and shouted for joy (see Job 38:7). And when Satan unleashed his anger against the Father and the Son and was cast out of heaven, *we were there,* fighting on the side of truth. In fact, President George Q. Cannon said that we "stood loyally by God and by Jesus, and . . . *did not flinch.*" (*Gospel Truth,* 7; emphasis added). We believed. We followed. And when we fought for truth in the most bitter of all confrontations, we did not flinch.

We were there. That means we existed. That means we were someone, that we as spirit children had identity and personality and the right to choose. Does it not therefore seem likely and logical that we had some kind of role in the premortal world before we came here? That we served each other and loved each other and led and taught and testified to each other? That we rallied and encouraged each other, and looked forward with enthusiasm to the high adventure of mortality? And that we were constantly learning and growing and preparing for the moment when our turn would arrive to embark upon our mortal sojourn?

Not only did we choose to follow Christ in the premortal world, but we qualified by virtue of our spiritual valor to be born into the House of Israel, which lineage President Harold B. Lee called the "most illustrious lineage" of all who would come to earth (*Ensign*, January 1974, 5). Elder Bruce R. McConkie wrote that "The whole house of Israel, known and segregated out from their fellows, was inclined toward spiritual things" (*The Mortal Messiah*, 1:23). He also noted that the foreordination to come to the earth as a member of the House of Israel was "an election, . . . for those so chosen, selected, or elected become, in this life, the favored people [in that] though all mankind may be saved by obedience, some find it easier to believe and obey than others" (*A New Witness for the Articles of Faith*, 512–13).

On the matter of being born into the House of Israel, President Lee elaborated: "Surely [this] must have been determined by the kind of lives we had lived in that premortal spirit world. Some may question these assumptions, but at the same time they will accept without any question the belief that each one of us will be judged when we leave this earth according to his or her deeds during our lives here in mortality. Isn't it just as reasonable to believe that what we have received here in this earth life was given to each of us according to the merits of our conduct before we came here?" (*Ensign*, January 1974, 5).

Now we are here, separated from the safety of our heavenly home, serving a mission in this lone and dreary world—a mission designed to prove whether or not we want to be part of the kingdom of God more than we want anything else. The Lord is testing our faith and our integrity to see if we will persevere in a realm where Satan reigns. Happily, despite taking this test in a turbulent era of mortality, we have once again chosen to follow Christ. The Lord was speaking of us when He said, "My sheep hear my voice, . . . and they follow me" (John 10:27). We have *heard* His voice because we *remember* and *recognize* His voice.

For we are among the elect whom the Lord has called during this "eleventh hour" to labor in His vineyard, a vineyard that "has become corrupted every whit" and in which only a few "doeth good" (D&C 33:3–4). God, who saw the "end from the beginning" (Abraham 2:8), foresaw perfectly what these times would demand.

George Q. Cannon repeatedly taught that God reserved his "noblest spirits" to come forth in this last dispensation (*Gospel Truth*, 1:8). "God has chosen us out of the world and has given us a great mission," he said. "I do not entertain a doubt myself but that we were selected and fore-ordained for the mission before the world was; that we had our parts allotted to us in this mortal state of existence as our Savior had his assigned to him" (*Juvenile Instructor*, 1 May 1887, 22:140). Further, he declared that the Lord saved for now those spirits who would have the "*courage* and

determination to face the world, and all the powers of the evil one,"
and who would "build up the Zion of our God, *fearless* of all consequences" (*Journal of Discourses,* 11:230; emphasis added).

Can you imagine that God, who knew us perfectly, reserved
us to come now, when the stakes would be higher and the opposition more intense than ever? Can you see that He sent *us* at a time
when He would need women who would raise and lead a righteous generation in the most lethal spiritual environment? Can
you imagine that He chose *us* because He knew we would be *fearless* in building Zion?

I can, because of what the Spirit has repeatedly whispered
about the sisters of this Church as I have sought the Lord in their
behalf while serving in the Relief Society general presidency.
Though we are sometimes far too casual about our spiritual
lives—though we get distracted by the world and live beneath
ourselves—the fact remains that *we have always been women of
God.* We have repeatedly made righteous choices, on both sides of
the veil, that demonstrate our faith and our faithfulness. We have
bound ourselves to the Lord with the most binding covenants of
mortality. We have been and are so much more valiant than we
think. We have so much more divine potential than we can comprehend.

The Lord told Abraham that he was among the "noble and
great ones" chosen for his earthly mission before he was born
(Abraham 3:22–23). And President Joseph F. Smith saw in vision
that *many* choice spirits reserved to come forth in this dispensation were also "among the noble and great ones" (D&C 138:53,
55). Elder Bruce R. McConkie said, "A *host* of mighty men and
equally glorious women comprised that group of 'the noble and

great ones.' . . . Can we do other than conclude that Mary and Eve and Sarah and *myriads* of our faithful sisters were numbered among them? Certainly these sisters . . . fought as valiantly in the War in Heaven as did the brethren, even as they in like manner stand firm . . . in mortality, in the cause of truth and righteousness" (*Sermons and Writings*, 198; emphasis added).

So what about us? Is it possible that *we* were among the noble and great? I believe it is more than possible, and that if we could even glimpse our premortal valor we wouldn't find it very difficult to keep the commandments and stay on the straight and narrow path here. The Prophet Joseph taught that "*every man* who has a calling to minister to the inhabitants of the world was ordained to that very purpose . . . before this world was" (*History of the Church*, 6:364). And President Spencer W. Kimball gave this additional insight: "Remember, in the world before we came here, faithful women were given certain assignments while faithful men were foreordained to certain priesthood tasks. While we do not now remember the particulars, this does not alter the glorious reality of what we once agreed to" (*Ensign*, November 1979, 102). I cannot imagine that we who have been called to bear and rear and nurture and teach and lead a chosen generation of children, youth, and women this late in the final dispensation were not among those deemed noble and great.

Noble and *great*. *Courageous* and *determined*. *Faithful* and *fearless*. That is who you are and who you have always been. And understanding it can change your life, because this knowledge carries a confidence that cannot be duplicated any other way.

Consider these words from Elder McConkie: "All Israel . . . have it in their power to gain exaltation; to be like the Son of

God, having gained his image; to be joint-heirs with him; to be justified and glorified; to be adopted into the family of God by faith; to be participators with their fathers in the covenant that God made with them; and to be inheritors, to the full, of the ancient promises. Implicit in all this is the fact that they are fore-ordained to be baptized, to join the Church, to receive the priest-hood, to enter the ordinance of celestial marriage, and to be sealed up unto eternal life" (*A New Witness for the Articles of Faith*, 513).

No wonder President Joseph F. Smith said during his min-istry, to the Relief Society sisters, "It is not for you to be led by the women of the world; it is for you to lead . . . the women of the world, in everything that is praise-worthy, everything that is God-like, everything that is uplifting and that is purifying to the chil-dren of men" (minutes of the General Board of the Relief Society, 17 March 1914, 54).

Sister Eliza R. Snow, the second general president of the Relief Society, said that her desire was that "we may as mothers and sisters in Israel teach and defend truth and righteousness, and sustain those who preach it. Every sister in this church should be a preacher of righteousness. . . . Let us be more energetic to . . . develop that strength of moral character which cannot be sur-passed on the face of the earth. . . . The circumstances in which we are placed and our positions in life demand this of us, because we have greater and higher privileges than any other females upon the face of the earth" (*Evening News*, 14 January 1870).

Despite such divine potential and lofty injunctions, I imag-ine most of us wonder, at least at times, if we're up to it all. I doubt many of us feel very noble or great. But then, neither did Enoch, who was stunned when the Lord called him into service: "Why is

it that I have found favor in thy sight, and am but a lad, and all
the people hate me; for I am slow of speech?" (Moses 6:31). The
Lord responded to Enoch by promising to walk with him and give
power to his words. Surely this encounter with the Lord gave
Enoch a new vision of himself. And the result was magnificent,
for so powerful was Enoch's word that when he "spake . . . the
earth trembled, and the mountains fled." Most important, his
people qualified to be taken up into heaven (Moses 7:13; see also
verses 18–21). But it happened *after* Enoch understood who he
was and that he had a sacred mission to perform.

Queen Esther came to understand something about fulfilling
her divine destiny. When she was chosen, because of her beauty, to
be the queen of King Ahasuerus, she elected not to reveal her
Jewish lineage. Later, when the king issued a decree to exterminate
the Jews, she and her people were in instant peril. It was after
Mordecai gave her a vision of her mission with these words, "who
knoweth whether thou art come to the kingdom for such a time as
this?" (Esther 4:14), that she stepped forward, revealed her nation-
ality, and obtained a reversal of the death decree.

The First Vision was all about identity—about the appearance of the Father and the Son to a boy whose sincere seeking
opened the heavens after centuries of darkness. Imagine what that
vision did to the teenage Joseph's sense of who he was and what
he had been called to do. Though it would yet be some years
before his mission as the Prophet of the Restoration began to
unfold in earnest, surely his image of himself changed instantly.
And three years later, feeling some concern about the weaknesses
to which he had succumbed during his youth, Joseph again petitioned the Lord, "that [he] might know of [his] state and standing

before him [meaning the Lord]" (JS–H 1:29). In other words, he wanted reassurance; he wanted to see himself as God did.

Saul, who made *sport* of persecuting Christians, was instantly converted after seeing the Savior and learning that he was a chosen vessel called to stand as a witness of Christ (see Acts 9:5; 22:15). There surely wasn't another Christian breathing who would have described Saul of Tarsus as "chosen"—at least not based on his earthly conduct. He must have been chosen before. And when Saul understood that, he changed his life and his name. The Apostle Paul's conversion was at least partly about coming to understand who he had always been.

As we increasingly come to understand the same thing, we will feel a greater sense of mission and more confidence living as women of God in a world that doesn't celebrate women of God. We will cheer each other on and lift others rather than compete with each other, because we'll feel secure in our own standing and status before the Lord. And we'll be eager to stand for truth, even when we must stand alone—for every consecrated, covenanted woman will have times when she must stand alone.

Satan of course knows how spiritually potent the knowledge of our divine identity is. He *hates* women of the noble birthright. He hates us because he is almost out of time, while we are en route to everlasting glory and a fulness of joy. He hates us because of the influence we have on husbands and children, family and friends, the Church and even the world. It is no secret to him that we are the Lord's secret weapon.

Thus it should not surprise us that the master of deceit is going all out to keep us from comprehending the majesty of who we are. He offers an array of seductive but sorry substitutes—

everything from labels and logos to titles and status—hoping to preoccupy us with the world's artificial identifiers. Not long ago a book listing *The 100 Most Influential Women of All Time* caught my attention. Mary, the mother of Christ, was mentioned—though not prominently. But Eve, the Mother of All Living, the woman without whom any of us wouldn't even be here, didn't even make the list. Come on! I won't reveal who was number one because I refuse to mention her name in the same context with Eve and Mary. This pitiful list demonstrates how absurd and skewed the world's view of women is—a view orchestrated by Satan.

In a prominent news magazine, a recent cover story titled "The Quest for Perfection" promoted a definition of perfection that was disgusting and, frankly, evil. It listed every available bodily lift, tuck, and augmentation, while not so much as mentioning virtues or values, marriage or motherhood or *anything,* for that matter, that matters to the Lord.

Clearly, Satan wants us to see ourselves as the world sees us, not as the Lord sees us, because the world's mirror, like a circus mirror in which a five-foot, ten-inch woman appears two feet tall, distorts and minimizes us. Satan tells us we're not good enough. Not smart enough. Not thin enough. Not cute enough. Not clever enough. Not *anything* enough. And that is a big, fat, devilish lie. He wants us to believe that there is no status or significance in being a mother. *That* is a lie—and an evil lie. He wants us to believe that the influence of women is inherently inferior. *And that is a lie.*

Yet *we* often buy into Satan's superficialities. After speaking in a general meeting on satellite, I received a letter that began, "Sister Dew, I can relate to you. I relate because I can see that you understand what it means to have a bad-hair day." Frankly, I've had *years* of bad-hair days. But though *we* don't always see beyond our hair and the labels on our clothing, the Lord does. For He "seeth not as man seeth; for man looketh on the outward appearance, but the Lord looketh on the heart" (1 Samuel 16:7).

Hence Satan's all-out attempt to prevent us from understanding how the Lord sees us, because the more clearly we understand our divine destiny, the more immune we become to Satan. When Satan tried to confuse Moses about his identity, saying, "Moses, *son of man,* worship me," Moses refused, responding: "*I am a son of God*" (Moses 1:12–13; emphasis added). He knew who he was because the Lord had previously told him, "Thou art my son; . . . And I have a work for thee" (Moses 1:4, 6). Surely one reason Moses was able to hold his ground with Satan while the great deceiver ranted and railed was because Moses knew clearly who he was.

So it is with us. We will never be happy or feel peace; we will never deal well with life's ambiguities; we will never live up to who we are as women of God until we overcome our mortal identity crisis by understanding *who we are, who we have always been, and who we may become.*

The Spirit is the key, for as President Joseph F. Smith taught, it is through the power of the Spirit that we may "catch a spark from the awakened memories of the immortal soul, which lights up our whole being as with the glory of our former home" (*Gospel Doctrine,* 14). It is the Spirit that allows us to pierce the veil and catch glimpses of who we are and who we have always been. Thus we need to be able to hear what the Lord through the Spirit has to say.

Asking in faith, fasting and praying, repenting regularly, forgiving and seeking forgiveness, worshiping in the temple where we may "receive a fulness of the Holy Ghost" (D&C 109:15), and being obedient all help us better hear the voice of the Lord in our minds and hearts (see D&C 8:2). Conversely, there are things we cannot do—movies and television programs we cannot watch, clothes we cannot wear, lyrics and music we cannot listen to, gossip we cannot spread, Internet sites we cannot visit, thoughts we cannot entertain, books we cannot read, and dishonesty we cannot tolerate—if we want the Spirit to be with us.

I can think of nothing more deserving of our energy than learning to better hear the voice of the Spirit. When the Nephite Twelve prayed for "that which they most desired," it was the gift of the Holy Ghost (3 Nephi 19:9). Why? Because the Holy Ghost "will show unto [us] all things" (2 Nephi 32:5), including who we are. I know this is true.

One day while rocking a niece who was then three months old, I was overwhelmed with an impression about the valor of her spirit. My tears flowed as I rocked and wondered just *whom* I was rocking. Now that my niece is older, I have told her about that experience, hoping to encourage her onward.

Similarly, when I was that shy farm girl, both Mother and Grandma often told me that there was something chosen about me and my generation. I couldn't quite imagine it, but my spirit wanted me to believe. So, in spite of my many insecurities, I quietly hung on their words and hoped they were true. Is there anything more meaningful a mother or any of us can do for the youth we love than to help them begin to see who they really are?

I heard a young man say just prior to departing for the

mission field that he hadn't wanted to serve a mission until he received his patriarchal blessing and realized for the first time that the Lord knew him and was counting on him. In other words, he saw a glimpse of who he has always been.

How many of us don't understand the simple principles C. S. Lewis expressed in his oft-quoted statement that "it is a serious thing to live in a society of possible gods and goddesses, to remember that the dullest and most uninteresting person you talk to may one day be a creature which . . . you would be strongly tempted to worship. . . . It is in light of these overwhelming possibilities, it is with the awe and circumspection proper to them, that we should conduct all our dealings with one another. . . . There are no ordinary people. You have never talked to a mere mortal. Nations, cultures, arts, civilizations—these are mortal, and their life is to ours as the life of a gnat. But it is immortals whom we joke with, work with, marry, snub, and exploit—immortal horrors or everlasting splendours" (*The Weight of Glory*, 14–15).

Brigham Young said: "I want to tell you, each and every one of you, that you are well acquainted with God our heavenly Father, or the great Elohim. You are all well acquainted with Him, for there is not a soul of you but what has lived in His house and dwelt with Him year after year; and yet you are seeking to become acquainted with Him, when the fact is, you have merely forgotten what you did know. . . . There is not a person here to-day but what is a son or a daughter of that Being" (*Journal of Discourses*, 4:216). He taught on another occasion: "When we look upon the human face we look upon the image of our Father and God; there is a divinity in each person male and female; there is the heavenly, there is the divine" (*Journal of Discourses*, 9:291).

As vital as the knowledge of our divine potential is, however, it alone doesn't make mortality failsafe. President Harold B. Lee warned that "there are many who were foreordained . . . to a greater state than they have prepared themselves for here. Even though they might have been among the noble and great, . . . they may fail of that calling here in mortality" (*Ensign,* January 1974, 5). In other words, "many are called, but few are chosen" (D&C 121:40). And *we* do the choosing, because the sobering reality is that whether or not we live up to our premortal promises is entirely up to us.

But the effort required is well worth it, for if we could comprehend how majestic and glorious a righteous woman made perfect in the celestial kingdom will be, we would rise up and never be the same again. We would gladly take upon us the name of Christ (see Alma 46:15)—which means following Him, becoming like Him, and dedicating ourselves to Him and His work. Women of God who honor their covenants look differently, dress differently, respond to crisis differently, and act and speak differently from women who have not made the same covenants. Women of God who know who they are have unusual influence.

There is a shop in New York City that I visit when I am there. I don't much care for the shop's snobby atmosphere, but because they carry skirts long enough for a tall woman, I endure the experience. On a recent visit, I made plans to meet a friend at this shop, and when I walked through the door at the appointed hour, a saleswoman was already waiting for me. "Mizz Dew?" she said with a charming European accent.

"Yes," I responded with surprise.

"Follow me," she answered, "your friend is already down-stairs."

I had never had such a warm reception, and for the next hour my friend and I became acquainted with this delightful woman from eastern Europe. After a time, our new saleswoman friend unexpectedly said, "There is something different about you two. What is it?"

"Do you really want to know?" we asked, almost in unison. When she nodded yes, I said, "Sit down." For an hour we told her what made us different. Since then we've sent materials explaining more. And we've just sent her something else—missionaries who will call on her.

What does knowing who we are and who we have always been have to do with bearing witness and testifying of Jesus Christ? It has *everything* to do with our mandate to take the gospel to every nation, kindred, tongue, and people—not to mention to our families and the neighbors next door. Because once we understand who we really are, we are not only beholden to the Lord to help others discover the same truths, we cannot be restrained from doing so. If a missionary moment can unfold in a stuffy New York dress shop, it can happen anywhere. And it will happen as the joy of the gospel and the reality of our mission light our faces and energize our lives.

I know a woman who responded to a nonmember friend wanting to sell her cosmetics by saying, "You can give me a facial if I can talk about the gospel." Both agreed. There is no more persuasive missionary messenger than a woman of God who knows who she is, and who is thrilled with what she knows. And there is no more important missionary work we will ever do than that within our own families, as their conversion is our highest priority.

Our objective through all of this isn't to build a bigger church, it is to bless the lives of people—mothers and fathers, sons and daughters—who deserve to know who *they* are, who they have always been, and who they may become. Let's not make this harder than it needs to be. We can begin simply by praying for opportunities to serve and for ways to more fully live the gospel, for we will do more missionary work through our example than we ever will pounding a pulpit. Last year the sisters in an Arizona ward provided service, no strings attached, to a nonmember family whose infant son was undergoing open-heart surgery. Those simple acts of kindness launched a remarkable sequence of events, and that family has now been baptized and that mother, father, and their three sons are beginning to find out who *they* are.

Repeatedly President Gordon B. Hinckley has pleaded with us to "become a vast army with enthusiasm for this work" (*Ensign,* May 1999, 110). In the 2000 General Relief Society Meeting, I invited the sisters of the Church to look for missionary opportunities. And at the 2001 General Young Women Meeting, Sister Margaret D. Nadauld invited every young woman to reach out to one girl and bring her into full activity during the year. Within a week several of my teenage nieces had already made contacts with nonmember friends. In other words, they enlisted immediately in the army.

Can we do any less? If the women and young women of this Church would join together in this glorious work, we would become a vast, enthusiastic, irresistible part of the Lord's army.

None of us can reach everyone, but we can all reach

someone—and, over the course of a lifetime, many someones. The gospel kingdom will not move forward as it must until we as mothers and grandmothers and favorite aunts become full and eager participants.

My plea is that you enlist, and enlist *now*, in the Lord's army. And in doing so I make this promise: As soon as we, the sisters of the Church, commit fully to this work, it will explode in an unprecedented way because of our unique, nurturing influence and because of the spirit and influence that accompanies righteous women. It will flourish because children and youth who see their mothers and leaders fearless about sharing the gospel will do likewise.

I will take the challenge. Will you join with me? Ask the Lord to help you, and He will. Begin by reading D&C 138 and Abraham 3 about the noble and great ones, and ask the Lord to talk with you, through the Spirit, about *you*. When you understand, without equivocation, that *you* were chosen and reserved for now, and when you live in harmony with that mission and with the promises you made premortally, you'll be happier than you have ever been before. That is a promise.

Will you seek to remember, with the help of the Holy Ghost, who you are and who you have always been? Will you remember that you stood by our Savior without flinching despite the most difficult of opposition? Will you remember that you were reserved for now because you would have the *courage* and the *determination* to face the world at its worst and to help raise and lead a chosen generation? Will you remember the covenants you have made and the power they carry? Will you remember that you are noble and great and a potential heir of all our Father has? Will you remember that you are the daughter of the King?

God is our Father, and His Only Begotten Son is the Christ. We are Theirs. They have bought us with a price. We will be fearless in building up Zion, as we come to know who we are and who we have always been.

CHAPTER 4

LESSONS FROM THE
DUST BOWL

OUR HOMES AND FAMILIES ARE THE BEST PLACES TO
LEARN ABOUT LIFE, ABOUT LOVE, AND ABOUT THE LORD.
AND THE CHURCH FAMILY CAN ALSO PROVIDE A PLACE
OF REFUGE AND SECURITY FROM THE WORLD'S STORMS.

MY GRANDPARENTS HOMESTEADED our family farm on the great plains of Kansas in 1916. By the time I came along, they had survived tornadoes, hail the size of grapefruit, the Depression (which drove countless farmers from the unforgiving prairie), and the Dust Bowl.

I loved to hear Grandma talk about the "olden days," but far and away my favorite stories—ones that I asked to hear over and over again—were about the Dust Bowl, that unusual phenomenon that she and Grandpa, along with my father and uncle, somehow weathered in their little house on the prairie.

In 1931 the farmers in western Kansas enjoyed good rainfall and thus a fruitful harvest. But the next year the rain stopped. Day after day, week after week, and unfortunately month after month my grandparents looked heavenward, hoping for signs of moisture. But none came. As a result, some 300,000 square miles of prairie turned dry, then drier, and then to powdery dust.

On the Great Plains, the wind blows sideways. (It is *always* a bad-hair day in Kansas.) The perpetual wind, combined with no rain, spelled disaster. Those strong prairie winds would kick up huge clouds of dirt that Grandma said looked like mountains in the distance. Some days the dust was so heavy that if farmers or livestock were caught in the fields, they suffocated for lack of oxygen. The only protection for man or beast was to come inside where it was safe.

For several years running, Grandpa planted a crop only to have the tender plants suffocate from lack of water. The dirt was so thick and came in such waves that after a while dust banks—just like snow banks, but made of dirt—formed against sides of barns, fences, and anything that would catch the dirt and allow it to accumulate. On my grandparents' farm a dust bank against the side of the barn allowed them to walk right up onto the roof. It has been estimated that during one horrible storm alone—on May 11, 1934—more than 300 million tons of Midwest topsoil (or roughly the amount of earth dredged from the Panama Canal) blew away. Grandma told me that on days like that, the dust was so dense that it became dark in the middle of the day.

And it all happened because there was no water.

There are lessons to be learned from the Dust Bowl.

First, there are times when the only way to survive the elements is to seek safety inside. Grandma constantly urged Grandpa to keep an eye on the weather so that if the wind began to kick up, he could get home before conditions became dangerous.

In similar fashion, the best place for us to seek safety and security against the dangerous elements of society is also inside—meaning, inside the home and family. We all need "places of security" (Alma 49:5), as Captain Moroni phrased it when he directed the Nephites to build fortresses against the marauding Lamanites.

The family is the foundational unit of society and of the Church, and it can provide a kind of nurturing protection and security that no other institution can duplicate. Ideally, the family is a place where we may safely retreat, where we may safely be vulnerable, where we develop resilience and replenish our emotional supply, and where we are taught what is important, what is good, and where happiness really comes from.

No wonder the family "is central to the Creator's plan for the eternal destiny of His children," as the Proclamation on the Family declares (*Ensign,* November 1995, 102). As President Gordon B. Hinckley has written: "Society's problems arise, almost without exception, out of the homes of the people. If there is to be a reformation, if there is to be a change, if there is to be a return to old and sacred values, it must begin in the home, with parents instilling within children the virtues that will make them into strong, contributing members of society" (*Standing for Something,* 165).

Not only do husband and wife have a "solemn responsibility to love and care for each other and for their children," but "parents have a sacred duty to rear their children in love and righteousness" (*Ensign,* November 1995, 102). In other words, just as in the Dust Bowl, when the weather outside (physical, moral, and spiritual) gets stormy, the best place to find protection is inside the home and family.

Periodically over the last fifty years, the Gallup Poll has asked respondents, "What is the most important problem facing the country today?" In a recent iteration (1999), and for the first time in the history of that poll, concerns over ethics, morality, and family decline topped the list. One in six adults listed these as the country's most pressing problems, followed by concerns over violence, economy, gun control, and education (*Emerging Trends*, 21:7; September 1999, 1–2).

About that same time, the Relief Society general presidency had the privilege of hosting a luncheon in the honor of Mrs. Jehan Sadat, wife of Egypt's former president Anwar Sadat. When the lunch-table conversation turned to concerns in the schools, and in particular the tragic events at Columbine High in the Denver suburbs, a gentleman at the table opined that the problem was really a failure of law enforcement to control the situation. Immediately Mrs. Sadat interrupted the conversation, with words to this effect: "No, that is not the problem," she said. "The problem is in our homes. Too many parents don't know what is happening to their children. Too many have abdicated responsibility for teaching their children what is important."

More than twenty years ago, President Spencer W. Kimball declared that the time would come "when only those who believe deeply and actively in the family will be able to preserve their families in the midst of the gathering evil around us" (in Conference Report, October 1980, 3). The home is the ideal place to come in from the storm.

Second, persistent inclement weather builds character and strength, particularly when we help each other. Our little farm created hard, back-breaking work for everyone in the family: Grandma and Grandpa and their two sons. In those early days, my grandparents had only the Lord and their boys to rely on. But the combination of the Lord and a family working together for one goal was—and is—a successful pattern.

While writing the biography of President Ezra Taft Benson, I unexpectedly came across a piece of correspondence that had personal meaning. Written by Central States Mission President Sam Carpenter to then–Secretary of Agriculture Ezra Taft Benson, it mentioned, of all people, my grandparents. In part, it read: "In 1916 Brother and Sister Charles L. Dew moved into southwest Kansas where they took up a homestead. Today . . . they are farming many acres of land. For many years now they have been stalwart members of the Church. . . . During the past weekend . . . I looked over their farming operations and was thrilled with what I saw. West Kansas is truly marvelous country. But it is no place for a tenderfoot. It takes people who are strong both physically and spiritually to battle the farming conditions in that area. The Dew family has stuck it out through all of the troubles that they have had out there. . . . You would recognize them as the kind of family that has built the farming areas of this country, and you would be inspired by their strength and their testimonies" (Sam Carpenter to Ezra Taft Benson, 1 December 1959).

By the world's measure, my grandparents weren't remarkable in any way. They were "just" farmers. But they built a farm and a family that have stood the test of time—and in the process they established a pattern of hard work, virtue, and resilience that has blessed their posterity.

Life is no place for a tenderfoot, but the family can prepare, strengthen, and insulate its members to deal with whatever kind of weather comes.

Third, water sustains life. Plants need water. The earth needs water. And we need water. Without water, the earth literally blew away in the Dust Bowl. In like manner, without Living Water we will face eternal dissolution.

With this in mind, consider the remarkable interchange of the Savior with a Samaritan woman at Jacob's Well. When the Savior asked if He might have a drink, this woman expressed surprise that He would approach her of all people, a Samaritan woman, as the Jewish people and the Samaritans were not friendly with one another. Jesus responded in curious fashion: "If thou knewest the gift of God, and who it is that saith to thee, Give me to drink; thou wouldest have asked of him, and he would have given thee living water."

She responded, "From whence then hast thou that living water? Art thou greater than our father Jacob, which gave us the well, and drank thereof himself, and his children, and his cattle?"

The Savior's answer may have seemed like a riddle: "Whosoever drinketh of this water shall thirst again," he said, referring to the water in the well. "But whosoever drinketh of the water that I shall give him shall never thirst; but the water that I shall give him shall be in him a well of water springing up into everlasting life" (John 4:10–14).

The Living Water, or the healing, redeeming power of Jesus Christ, is as essential to our well-being here and hereafter as water is to plants or to the preservation of the earth or to the sustaining of our physical lives. Jesus Christ is that Living Water, and in Him reside the means for us to flourish here in mortality and to live eternally.

The family is the ideal place to learn how to drink of that Living Water.

Aside from our personal testimonies, which anchor us to Jesus Christ and His gospel, the most vital place of security on this earth is the family. President Howard W. Hunter called it "the most important unit in time and in eternity and, as such, [it] transcends every other interest in life" (*Ensign*, November 1994, 50).

Sociologists and family historians predict that the twenty-first century will bring a dramatic redefinition of the family—one that will almost certainly undermine what God intended it to be. But then, the Proclamation on the Family warns that "the disintegration of the family will bring upon [us] . . . the calamities foretold by ancient and modern prophets" (*Ensign*, November 1995, 102).

I have no doubt about the prime importance of home and family. About this issue the leaders of the Church have been abundantly clear—that "the family is ordained of God"; that "marriage between man and woman is essential to His eternal plan"; that "children are entitled to birth within the bonds of matrimony, and to be reared by a father and a mother who honor marital vows with complete fidelity"; and that "happiness in family life is most likely to be achieved when founded upon the teachings of the Lord Jesus Christ" *(Ensign*, November 1995, 102).

In a letter to members of the Church throughout the world dated February 11, 1999, the First Presidency said that "the home is the basis of a righteous life, and no other instrumentality can take its place or fulfill its essential functions."

Although many in the world may have long since dismissed some of these principles as medieval and even unrealistic, the fact remains that the family is the Lord's organization for most effectively nurturing His children. It is the best institution for rearing responsible men and women. It is the only organization that can truly teach, lead, love, and care for children as the Lord would have them cared for.

And yet we see everywhere polarized views regarding the family, gender, marriage, and the rearing of children, as well as evidence of the disintegration, dissolution, and destruction of the family. The statistics on issues related to the family are compelling: children who don't live with both parents are more likely to grow up poor, have problems in school, get into trouble with the law, and have health and emotional disorders (see *Standing for Something,* 147).

The *Wall Street Journal* published the results of a two-year study sponsored by the Council on the Family in America in 1995: "American society would be better off if more people got married and stayed married" (*Standing for Something,* 146). It's interesting that it took a two-year study to corroborate what the Lord has taught again and again in the scriptures and through the mouths of prophets and apostles.

We as women have unique and vital roles to play in protecting and defending the family. President Gordon B. Hinckley was speaking to us when he declared that "the home is under siege. So many families are being destroyed. . . . If anyone can change the dismal situation into which we are sliding, it is you. Rise up, O women of Zion, rise to the great challenge which faces you. . . . My challenge to you . . . is that you will rededicate yourselves to the strengthening of your homes" *(Ensign,* November 1998, 99–100).

Two years later President Hinckley spoke again to the sisters of the Church: "You have nothing in this world more precious than your children. When you grow old, when your hair turns white and your body grows weary, when you are prone to sit in a rocker and meditate on the things of your life, nothing will be so important as the question of how your children have turned out. . . . The searing question that will cross your mind again and again will be, How well have my children done? If the answer is that they have done very well, then your happiness will be complete. If they have done less than well, then no other satisfaction can compensate for your loss" (*Ensign*, November 2000, 97).

If the world can't look to us for a clear signal about the sanctity of marriage, motherhood, and the family, where can it look? This statement from President Heber J. Grant is classic: "The mother in the family far more than the father, is the one who instills in the hearts of the children, a testimony and love for the gospel . . . ; and wherever you find a woman who is devoted to this work, almost without exception you will find that her children are devoted to it" (*Gospel Standards*, 101).

Research conducted by the Church indicates that the single biggest factor affecting a child's participation in and attendance at church is the mother's attendance. This is not to say that the father's activity and participation are unimportant, but it is principally mothers who help their children prepare talks for Primary, who make sure their youth make it to girls camp and Mutual and youth conference, who help their children get ready on Sunday morning. Mothers are the emotional glue that holds the family together. President Joseph F. Smith said: "There are people fond of saying that women are the weaker vessels. I don't believe it. Physically, they may be; but spiritually, morally, . . . and in faith, what man can match a woman who is really convinced?" (quoted in Widtsoe, *Priesthood and Church Government*, 86).

As women, our physical endurance is not as great as that of men. But women bring a remarkable strength to the family that is both distinct and irreplaceable.

Though there are those who will disagree, I acknowledge my belief that there is nothing a woman can do that is more significant than rearing children to live righteous, contributing, faith-filled lives. I believe it not only because of the teachings of prophets and apostles but because of what I have experienced and observed. I can think of nothing a woman can do in a board room, at a conference table, or in front of a camera that begins to equate with helping shape someone's life, with helping someone else do what he or she has come here to do.

Women, beginning with mothers, are uniquely stationed at the crossroads of the lives of youth and children—as well as many others—and are in a position, day in and day out, to teach and model virtues and values.

And clearly, there are certain values that are best taught, modeled, and reinforced in the home. Here are just a few:

1.

First, *teach your children to tell the truth*. Abigail Adams, the wife of President John Adams, wrote her friend Mercy Otis Warren that the first thing she should instill in her children was "a sacred regard for Veracity" because it makes "everything else come easier" (quoted in *Spirit of America*, 233). Honesty has become increasingly difficult to teach, as the conduct of many in the public eye has made the virtue of integrity seem outmoded and unrewarded. And yet, do you care if the principal of your son's high school tells the truth? Or your investment banker? Or your insurance adjustor? Or the circuit court judge hearing your case? Or the fellow selling you a car? Honesty and integrity are the threads that weave the fabric of society together, and the best laboratory for learning and practicing these virtues is within the family.

2. *Teach children the benefit and blessings of moral virtue.* It is curious that so many today feel that morality is antiquated, for I have yet to meet the man or woman who is happier because of adultery, infidelity, or other breaches of integrity. Immorality breeds not only disease but discontent, a lack of self-respect, and anxiety. And immorality devastates the family. Our youth don't get that picture at school, in the movies, or from their peers, however, where too often they see sex exploited, celebrated, and encouraged. Immorality is the most offensive kind of dishonesty, and the best chance our youth have of learning this in a society intoxicated with sexuality is from us, as we *show* them the virtue of having virtue. This leads to the next point best learned at home.

3. *Teach your children to have confidence in standing up for what they believe.* I think of a teenage niece who declined the invitation to attend a party at a friend's home because she knew there would be R-rated movies shown there. Not wanting to make it an issue with her friend, she simply said she couldn't attend. But the friend persisted, until my niece quietly explained that she didn't want to impose her beliefs on anyone else, but that she wouldn't be comfortable in a situation where rough movies were shown. My niece's friend asked if she would select the movies for the evening. The problem was solved, and everyone benefited.

4. *Teach your children to serve and care more about others than themselves.* When my nephew Tanner completed his Eagle Scout

project, having arranged for more than 500 school kits to benefit humanitarian services, I called him to say, essentially, "Way to go!" His instant reply was, "You should tell Mom way to go, because I never would have made it without her." No doubt every mother of an Eagle Scout relates to this. So often, mothers are the ones who help their children experience the joy of doing something for someone other than themselves.

5. *Teach your children to work* and to recognize that there is a sense of fulfillment in honest work and a job well done.

6. *Teach them to have tolerance for others who are different*, without surrendering their own values. President Hinckley has told about uttering a racial slur as a boy, at which point his mother promptly washed his mouth out with soap. The point was made, and he never forgot it.

7. *Teach your children to forgive*, and that it is possible to solve almost every problem if you can learn to both apologize and accept an apology. These skills are best modeled by parents who are willing to ask for and extend forgiveness—particularly with their children.

8. *Teach them to love to learn* and to master their talents. Again, President Hinckley has often described his modest childhood home as having a library filled with books. His parents loved reading, and that was the beginning of his own lifelong fascination with books and reading. He still refers to a set of *Harvard Classics*, a prized possession from his father's library.

9. *Teach your children to be kind*, and that there is nothing ever gained by anger, by unfair accusation, or by hurting someone else.

10. *Teach them to love life* and to find joy and adventure in the journey.

Teach them the difference between right and wrong. Parents and other adult members of the family are in an ideal position to make it fashionable again to be good and to do good—to live exemplary moral lives.

Teach your children the sanctity of marriage. I love what John Adams wrote to his beloved wife, Abigail: "I must intreat you, my dear Partner in all the Joys and Sorrows, Prosperity and Adversity of my Life, to take a Part with me in the Struggle" (quoted in *Spirit of America*, 290). Teach your children—by example—that marriage can make "the struggle" easier, rather than be "the struggle" itself.

A colleague, a man of considerable professional accomplishment, told me one day that women have more influence on men than men have on men. I questioned him about this, but he insisted, "Compliments or kindness sound and feel different to a man when they come from a woman; they mean something different and have a different kind of impact." And then he added, "*No one* has more influence on me than my wife."

Teach your children how valuable they are—to you and to the Lord. Grandma used to take me with her everywhere. Just the fact that she wanted me with her made me feel important. I loved hearing her introduce me to someone new with words as simple as, "This is my eldest granddaughter, Sheri. Aren't I lucky to have her with me today?"

Teach your children that virtue leads to happiness, and that the commandments are guidelines to keep us within the path that leads to joy.

Teach them to love being obedient, and that there are consequences for being disobedient.

Teach them to love the scriptures, and that the scriptures are a conduit for personal revelation. As in all things, parents are the best teachers. If children can see that the people they respect love the scriptures, at some point they'll give them a try.

Teach them how to pray and to fast, and that fasting and prayer connect them with the heavens and draw upon a kind of power that transcends anything earthly.

Teach them how to hear the voice of the Lord. Talk to them about it. Help them identify the stirrings of the Holy Ghost. I think of a friend who took her eight-year-old grandson to a temple dedication. When the choir sang "The Spirit of God Like a Fire Is Burning" combined with the "Hosanna Anthem" at the conclusion, the boy turned to his grandmother and said that he could feel something through his entire body. Later she took the opportunity to tell him that what he had felt was the Holy Ghost.

Teach your children to love the Lord more than the world, more than their friends, more than anyone. Once again, this is best taught by example. If children see their parents devoted to the Lord, they are likely to follow that same path.

Now, lest you become frustrated and give up, wondering if it is possible to teach all of these things in your family, take heart. We don't have to do it all at once, and we don't have to do it alone. The Lord will help us, as will friends, leaders, and teachers, but the family—including the extended family—is the best arena for these kinds of virtues and values to take root and then begin to grow.

In so many ways, teaching values and principles begins with us, the women of the family—mothers and grandmothers, but also sisters, nieces, and aunts. It begins with the way we live, with what we model for our children and grandchildren, our sisters and nieces. Do we tell the truth? Do we bring refinement and strength and optimism and kindness and nurturing to the family? There are few things more unappealing than a coarse, overexposed, immodest, deceitful woman. And there are few things more delightful and appealing than a woman of integrity, grace, strength, and conviction who blesses those she loves.

I have a friend, a distinguished educator, who was raised by his widowed mother. She had just two dresses, one for weekdays and one for Sunday. The Sunday dress never came out during the week. When my friend ran in his high school election for student-body president and won, he wanted his mother at the assembly where his election would be announced, but he was worried that she would come wearing her weekday dress. The morning of the assembly, he kept scanning the crowd for his mother, but couldn't find her. Then later, as he was giving his acceptance speech, he saw her, wearing her weekday dress but standing behind the bleachers where she couldn't be seen. He knew instinctively that she had sensed his discomfort about having her there, yet neither could she stay away. "I will never forget that moment," he says. "I was so ashamed of myself. And yet I learned something I have never forgotten: that in my mother I had a true champion, someone who believed in me completely and would never let me down. I also learned that she cared a lot more about my feelings than she did her own. Having her there was more important than the entire cheering student body."

We as women can help those we love do more and be more than they thought they could do or be on their own. Our nurturing helps create a sense of belonging. We all have a longing to belong, and hence our fascination with logos and brands and teams and clubs. But the most important place we can belong—the place that has greatest influence on our moral, emotional, and spiritual development—is the family.

Just because I have not had the privilege of bearing children does not mean that I am unconcerned about the family, for we are all responsible to help rear and lead a chosen generation. I have a family that includes seventeen nieces and nephews, and I work very hard at being their favorite aunt. Though I would do anything for these children, I have often wondered just who is helping whom. I will never forget one such experience.

In the early spring of 1999 I received an assignment to speak at the April general conference. Such an assignment is both a privilege and a pressure, and it took me many weeks of hard work to complete the message I had felt prompted to prepare.

But then, just days before conference, I came to understand that the talk I had prepared was not the one I should deliver on Easter Sunday. It seemed inconceivable to start over, but that was what I had to do. I had just three days to prepare an entirely new address—something that looked nothing short of impossible. After having slaved day and night for weeks on the first message, I was emotionally, physically, and spiritually spent.

All of this transpired on a Friday, so I went home, opened my scriptures, turned on my computer, and basically went brain dead. All afternoon, all through the night, and all the next day I worked—or tried to work. But by Saturday evening I had nothing but a floor littered with dozens of crumpled wads of paper to show for my work. I was exhausted. I was depressed. I had no ideas. The Spirit seemed to have vanished. And fear was gripping every cell of my body. Late Saturday evening I decided to lie down for a few hours.

Then something happened unlike anything I have experienced before with relation to preparing a talk. When I arose at 3:00 A.M. Sunday morning, after what was little more than a good nap, I felt optimistic and full of energy. I again turned on my computer, opened my scriptures, and began to write. Some crumpled-up wads of paper still hit the floor, but nine hours later the talk was done. Parting the Red Sea would have been no more miraculous to me.

Now, for the rest of the story. When my two sisters had learned about my plight on Friday evening, they had sprung into action, contacting everyone in our family and asking them to fast, beginning Saturday at noon. "We'll get all of your nieces and nephews fasting for you. That will work," they said.

When I felt clear-headed and rejuvenated Sunday morning, and as ideas for the talk began to come, I had the impression that I was being strengthened beyond any normal capability because of the fasting and prayers of my family, and perhaps particularly because of nieces and nephews willing to help their Aunt Sheri. I have never experienced such a restoration of mind and spirit in so short a period of time. I simply could not have done what I had to do if my family had not united to call upon the Lord in my behalf.

What if our parents had not taught us to fast and pray as children? And what if my siblings hadn't continued this pattern in their own homes? But everyone was ready and willing to respond when I was in need. No one had to be "taught" how to fast for this emergency. Fasting and praying as a family, and even as an extended family, was standard operating procedure. Even Natalie, who was then just seven, completed for her first time a full twenty-four-hour fast, because she "knew Aunt Sheri needed help." And did she ever!

My family provided a welcome safety net during a time of great challenge—a place to come in from the storm.

The foundation of the Church and the hope of the future are in the family, and there is no place of security like it. There is power in the family that we will find nowhere else, a power that spans generations and reaches across the veil.

My Grandma Dew's last written words were addressed to her priesthood leader asking to be released from her calling because she had become so ill. She wrote, "I hope the Lord does not think I have said no to Him. I love the gospel so very much and also this work." Grandma died one week later. But she left behind a legacy of faith that has had a profound influence on me.

Grandma was a prolific genealogist, but she failed to keep a journal—or so I thought. Then, not long ago, one of my sisters came across a brief life history wherein Grandma had recounted some of the events of her life, including the loss of her eldest son. About that incident she wrote, "This has been a very hard thing for us to take. It has left such a great vacancy that cannot be filled in this life. But because the sealing power of the gospel is upon the earth and because we did have our sons sealed to us in the temple, we do have hope that they, with their families, will be ours for eternity."

The tenderness of that passage notwithstanding, the poignant aspect of this entry is contained in the next sentence, where Grandma wrote, simply, "The Lord has been good to us."

The juxtaposition of her faith in the Lord with the painful reflection of her son's loss spoke volumes to me, her eldest granddaughter.

Then, continuing, I found that she had written something to me—or at least it felt as though it had been written to me: "I wish to say, for the benefit of our posterity who may read this history, whatever you do, work with as much determination to secure enough to keep you for the eternity. Do not be slack in your duties. The gospel is true. We must always be found defending it. But yea more, we must be found teaching it, by word and something much more noticeable, by our every action. We are children of God, but to be a joint-heir with Jesus Christ, we must take into our lives the attributes he had."

Through her words, it felt as though Grandma had reached through the veil to talk directly to me—again. Though she has been gone more than thirty-five years, her lingering influence has been immeasurable. Sometimes the image of her standing at a pulpit teaching the gospel keeps me going. Her faith strengthens mine. I want her to be proud of me. And I am trying to live as she lived, though that is a tall order.

Yes, our eternal families provide a vital place of security—a place to come in from the storm; a place to build character and strength, for life is no place for a tenderfoot; and a place to learn how to drink of the Living Water from which we will never thirst.

In addition to the nuclear family, the Church family provides a solid place of security. As individuals and families we need additional protection from the storms of the world, as spelled out in a revelation Joseph Smith received on April 26, 1838: "That the gathering together upon the land of Zion, and upon her stakes, may be for a defense, and for a refuge from the storm, and from wrath when it shall be poured out without mixture upon the whole earth" (D&C 115:6).

The Lord made it known early to the Saints in this dispensation that it was His will that all who would call on His name and worship Him according to His everlasting gospel "should gather together, and stand in holy places" (D&C 101:22). In addition, there are many members of the Church whose immediate and even extended family are not members of the Church—individuals who are not able to go home and talk with a spouse or children or siblings about the gospel and thus find reinforcement. Hence the reason that the stakes of Zion, meaning the Church family, can provide a defense and a refuge from the storm for all weary, worthy travelers along the road of life.

I have experienced this for myself, for as much as I love my family and depend upon them, life would seem empty were it not for my Church family. I have often been asked why I feel so comfortable as a never-married member in such a family-oriented Church.

I do not understand this question, which implies that I would be happier if I were not a member of the Church. It also implies that happiness comes only to those whose lives are ideal, which would make, incidentally, for a very small group of happy people. So perhaps the question on some people's minds is really, How does someone in nontraditional circumstances feel a sense of belonging in The Church of Jesus Christ?

The answer has been articulated repeatedly by President Hinckley when he has identified the three things each new member—and may I suggest *each member*—of the Church needs:

friends, a responsibility (or meaningful opportunities to serve), and the privilege of being taught by the Spirit, or nurtured by the good word of God (see *Ensign*, May 1999, 108).

As I have reflected on my experience in the Church and on the reasons I have felt so at home within this divinely inspired organization, I have concluded that it is because I have been blessed to have these three essential ingredients since the time I was young.

To begin with, my dearest friends, with few exceptions, have come into my life as a result of our service together in the Church. Most of these friends hail from backgrounds far different from mine. Most are married. Most have children. Many have grandchildren. We have laughed together and enjoyed each others' successes, and we have cried together and shared pain and disappointment. Through it all I have come to find, gratefully, that marital status, background, and life circumstances have almost nothing to do with friendship. I can't imagine where I would be were it not for the friends who have come into my life *as a direct result* of active participation in all levels of Church service.

Likewise, I began as a young girl to have opportunities to serve in our small branch, where each of us was called upon frequently to speak, teach, lead the singing, and play the piano. I was barely sixteen when I was first called to serve in a presidency, as second counselor in our branch's Primary presidency. I don't remember much about that experience, and I don't suppose I did a very good job. But I felt needed, and I began to learn what presidencies do and how they function. Similar opportunities have continued to the present day, my marital status notwithstanding. I will be forever grateful to the stake president who called me to serve as the Relief Society president in a stake where nearly every other woman was married. In my call he sent a message—to me and to my sisters—that what we have in common is far more important than any circumstantial life differences we may have.

If there is anywhere in the world where every one of us, regardless of our personal circumstances, should feel accepted, needed, valued, and loved, it is within our Church family. And every one of us can reach out to others and help them feel a sense of belonging.

The Lord intended for us to take care of each other. We all must work out our salvation on our own, but there is no reason we should have to do it alone! How, after all, did the Savior spend His last hours in mortality? He dined with His trusted friends, His disciples. He washed their feet, filthy from the dusty streets of Jerusalem. He counseled them. And He gave them hope for the days ahead while articulating His expectation of His followers: "A new commandment I give unto you, That ye love one another; as I have loved you. . . . By this shall all men know that ye are my disciples, if ye have love one to another" (John 13:34–35). Indeed, as President Joseph F. Smith taught, the "test . . . of our soul's greatness is . . . to be sought in our ability to comfort and console, our ability to help others, rather than in our ability to help ourselves and crowd others down in the struggle of life" (*Gospel Doctrine,* 265).

Within our Church structure, the Lord in His wisdom and mercy has provided many opportunities—through visiting teaching and home teaching, through leading and teaching, through unending calls to render compassionate service—for us to learn how to put someone else's needs ahead of our own.

It matters not that our personal circumstances differ. Some struggle with illness from infancy, while others are robust until the day they die. Some feel the sting of divorce or the sudden loss of a loved one; others deal with the debilitating effects of addiction or the regret and disappointment of missed opportunities. Some are married and juggle large households; others wish they had husbands and posterity to complicate their lives. It doesn't matter that we have not experienced each other's woes. What does matter is our reservoir of compassion and our testimonies born of experience that the Lord is the ultimate Healer and Source of peace. What we have in common—including our values, our goals, our ultimate potential, and the covenants we have made—is so much more important than the incidental life details that distinguish and too often separate us from each other.

If for nothing else than an expression of gratitude for the Savior's resplendent gift, can we help and care for each other? Imagine the cumulative, magnifying, multiplying effect if each one of us helped strengthen just one or two others during the next twelve months. It would be impossible to measure the influence— for those we help, and for us as well. It is as an angel told Paul while on his perilous journey to Rome: "Fear not. . . . God hath given thee all them that sail with thee. Wherefore, . . . be of good cheer" (Acts 27:24–25). The Lord has given us each other. He doesn't intend us to sail through this life alone.

I will never forget the first time I spoke from the Tabernacle pulpit in a general meeting. I had prepared for weeks. I had fasted and prayed. But as my turn to speak approached, I began to have what could only be described as a meltdown. I had expected to be nervous, but the "terror of the Tabernacle" was far worse than anything I had imagined. At one point, I literally couldn't breathe. As I pleaded silently with the Lord for help, I mentioned that it would be important to be able to get air into my lungs when I stepped to the pulpit.

And then, just moments before I stood to speak, an unexpected image came to mind. It was of a group of sisters in Montreal, Canada, where I had visited a few weeks earlier. They had promised to pray for me at this meeting, and I knew they were keeping their promise, for a feeling of total and immediate calm washed over me.

Not long thereafter when a friend visited Montreal, I asked her to tell the Relief Society president of the Montreal French-speaking stake that she and her sisters had made all the difference for me that night. Upon hearing the story this woman exclaimed, "We just knew she knew that we were praying for her!"

Do we understand how sustaining relationships communicated by the Spirit can be? Do we understand the strength of righteous sisters caring for one another? That night, the concern and caring of sisters from another country whom I had met but once made all the difference.

The Lord intended for us to mean a lot to each other—both within our families and within the Church family. Both kinds of family provide places of security where we may come in from the storm. They teach us character and instill the values that enable us to deal with the rugged environment around us. And they teach us how to drink from that Living Water that will quench our thirst eternally.

CHAPTER 5

THIS IS A TEST;
IT IS ONLY A TEST

WE CAN EXPECT TO ENCOUNTER OBSTACLES
THROUGHOUT OUR MORTAL SOJOURN—MANY OF THEM
INSPIRED BY THE ADVERSARY, WHO IS DETERMINED TO
DERAIL, DISCOURAGE, DEPRESS, DISHEARTEN,
DEMEAN, DISAPPOINT, AND DECEIVE US.

MOM MADE ME TAKE PIANO LESSONS. And because I am her eldest, and she had not yet been worn down by the thankless task of prodding five children to practice every day, my whining about hating to practice fell on deaf ears. The fact that I eventually studied piano for fifteen years is largely a tribute to Mother's resilience and endurance. I wish I had a dollar for every time she prophesied that I would thank her one day for all of the musical torture. As always, she was right. I have thanked her, again and again, for that introduction to the keyboard, because somewhere between those first bars of "Here we go, up a row, to a birthday party" and *The Warsaw Concerto,* I fell in love with music, especially classical music, which in its more magnificent passages made my heart feel like it was going to leap out of my chest—in other words, it made my young spirit soar.

Here, again, Mother deserves all the credit. I couldn't have been more than ten or eleven when she gave me a stack of classical albums (yes, I am old enough to remember albums), introducing me to some of the great composers whose works were characterized by dramatic musical passages and what I call the Big Finish.

I would lie in front of the stereo for hours, listening to the third movement of Rachmaninoff's *Second Piano Concerto* or his *Prelude in C# Minor,* all the while imagining myself at a shiny black concert grand in Carnegie Hall. I pictured my debut there, standing ovation and all. I imagined that I would be humble but brilliant—brilliant enough to move an entire audience, including Mother, to tears. Somewhere in all of my daydreaming, I caught a vision of how it would feel to play so beautifully that others' hearts would soar.

At that point, Mother no longer had to encourage me to practice. Once I had a vision of the possibilities, the motivation to master the piano came from inside me. Do I mean to suggest that practicing became magically enjoyable? Absolutely not! It was more often sheer drudgery than not. But I found a technique that helped me endure those tedious hours of practice, day in and day out. When I set out to tackle a new piece, I would master and memorize the Big Finish first, all the while visualizing myself in concert, where the audience jumped to its feet at the last chord. Imagining how grand the Big Finish would be—especially at Carnegie Hall—kept me going through months of rehearsal on technical passages that didn't provide nearly the same sense of drama but that had to be mastered nonetheless.

In short, my progress on the piano and my motivation to practice increased dramatically when *I* caught a vision of my potential.

We are temporarily afflicted with the amnesia of mortality. But just as my spirit was stirred by the majesty of those dramatic musical passages and the possibility of performing them flawlessly, it is *the* Spirit that also sheds light upon our ultimate potential— which is the grandest finish of all.

If, on the other hand, we are not able to catch a vision of the Big Finish—meaning a clear image of who we are, who we have always been, and who we are becoming—we most likely will not be willing to practice. Life, like classical music, is full of difficult passages that are conquered as much through endurance and determination as through any particular skill.

Remember the announcements that used to interrupt your regularly scheduled television programming? "This is a test of the emergency broadcasting system. It is only a test. If this were a real emergency, you would be notified through this station." You've probably seen the poster that reads, "Life is a test. It is only a test. Had this been a real life, you would have been instructed where to go and what to do." It reminds me of a greeting card that sums up my feelings when life seems punctuated with problems: "Mother told me there would be days like this . . . But she failed to mention they could go on for months [and I would add, years] at a time."

There are times when days feel like months and when life feels like the test that it is, days when the vision and hope of a Big Finish are dimmed by immediate demands and pressures and disappointments, days when one might wish for a more manageable mortal exam.

For indeed, this life *is* a test. It is only a test—meaning, that's *all* it is. Nothing more, but nothing less. It is a test of many things—of our convictions and priorities, our faith and our faithfulness, our patience and our resilience, and, in the end, our ultimate desires. In the long run, as Alma taught, whatever we truly desire, we will have. "I know that [God] granteth unto men according to their desire . . . ; yea, I know that he allotteth unto men . . . according to their wills, whether they be unto salvation or unto destruction" (Alma 29:4).

Thankfully, our experience here is an open-book test. The purpose of our lives isn't a secret, guarded under lock and key until the Divine Schoolmaster reveals the answers. We know why we're here, and we have received from prophets ancient and modern an extensive set of instructions that never become passé or grow outdated.

Yes, life *is* a test—of many things. But at the risk of sounding simplistic, may I suggest that the mortal experience is largely about vision—our vision of ourselves and our ultimate Big Finish. And vision is determined by faith. The firmer our faith in Jesus Christ, the clearer our vision of ourselves and what we can ultimately achieve and become.

A vision of our potential destination and the road to get there is central to survival—both spiritually and physically. Consider Lehi and his family. Imagine the family home evening when he informed his wife and children that the Lord had directed them to pack a few belongings and foray into the wilderness, leaving behind their life of comfort. I doubt any of them were enthusiastic about the news. Can't you just hear the dialogue?

"You want us to do *what?* To throw a few things in a bag and leave home?"

"Yes, that is what the Lord has asked us to do."

"Where are we going?"

"Well, I'm not entirely sure. I know only that we must leave Jerusalem. And by the way, we'll need to travel light. So leave most of your things here."

"How soon will we be coming back home?"

"Well . . . that isn't entirely clear. Perhaps never."

We know how Laman and Lemuel responded, initially and in perpetuity: with sulky and often sinful behavior. Why didn't Nephi, their younger (and presumably less mature) brother, react the same way? He probably wasn't thrilled with his father's news either.

The difference is a classic demonstration of the power of vision. While Laman and Lemuel resisted and rebelled, Nephi asked the Lord if he might see what his father had seen. He had the faith to seek his own vision. "I, Nephi, . . . did cry unto the Lord; and behold he did visit me, and did soften my heart that I did believe all the words which had been spoken by my father; wherefore, I did not rebel against him like unto my brothers" (1 Nephi 2:16). That vision, or sense of purpose, sustained Nephi through a life of trial and tribulation. It helped him pass the test, so to speak.

In similar fashion, from the time he announced that he had seen the Father and the Son until he died a martyr, Joseph Smith endured constant persecution. How did he do it? Let us never forget that his prophetic mission began with a vision. Said he with certitude and conviction, "I have actually seen a vision; and who am I that I can withstand God, or why does the world think to make me deny what I have actually seen? For I had seen a vision; I knew it, and I knew that God knew it, and I could not deny it, neither dared I do it; at least I knew that by so doing I would offend God, and come under condemnation" (JS–H 1:25).

In time the Prophet Joseph came to realize why he seemed to be the object of so much of the adversary's attention: "It seems as though the adversary was aware, at a very early period of my life, that I was destined to prove a disturber and an annoyer of his kingdom; else why should the powers of darkness combine against me? Why the opposition and persecution that arose against me, almost in my infancy?" (JS–H 1:20). No doubt that vision or understanding of what he was experiencing, and why, helped Joseph endure the test.

"Where there is no vision, the people perish," Solomon proclaimed (Proverbs 29:18). And perhaps nothing is more vital today than having a vision, manifest by the Spirit, of who we are, of who we have always been, and of who we can become; of our intrinsic value to the Lord; and of the unparalleled role we have the opportunity of playing in these latter days. We are literally the offspring of God, with the potential of exaltation (see Acts 17:29; D&C 76:24). "The Spirit itself beareth witness with our spirit, that we are the children of God: and if children, then heirs; heirs of God, and joint-heirs with Christ" (Romans 8:16–17).

But how do *we* get a clear vision of who we are and where we are and where we may ultimately go? How do we gain an eternal perspective compelling enough to move us to action and to govern our choices and priorities? From whence cometh the vision?

As Lehi and his family learned, their Liahona worked according to their faith in God (see Alma 37:40). When they became slothful in their devotions and ceased to exercise faith, the marvelous works ceased. This is in keeping with divine law, for, as Elder James E. Talmage taught, "Faith is of itself a principle of power; and by its presence or absence, . . . even the Lord was and is influenced, and in great measure controlled, in the bestowal or withholding of blessings" (*Jesus the Christ,* 318). Therefore, let us not "be slothful because of the easiness of the way. . . . The way is prepared, and if we will look we may live forever" (Alma 37:46).

One would think it would be easy to embrace and have faith in the gift of the Atonement. But I fear that some of us understand just enough about the gospel to feel guilty—guilty that we are not measuring up to some undefinable standard—but not enough about the Atonement to feel the peace and strength, the power and mercy, it affords us.

Perhaps some of us don't understand and therefore don't appreciate the magnificence of the doctrines of the gospel of Jesus Christ. Perhaps therefore we don't know how to draw the power of the Atonement into our lives. Others seem unwilling to seek its blessings. And some don't ask because they don't feel worthy. It's quite the irony—that the gospel of the great Jehovah, which contains the power to save every human being and to strengthen every soul, is sometimes interpreted in such a way that feelings of inadequacy result.

Truman G. Madsen has said it this way: "The cruelest thing you can do to a human being is to make him forget that he or she is the son or daughter of a king." There is a direct relationship between our personal experience with the Lord and how we see ourselves. The closer we grow to him, the more clear and complete becomes our vision of who we are, who we have always been, and who we may become.

I have tender feelings about the connection between our faith in the Lord and the way we see ourselves because I have spent much of my life struggling to feel that I measured up. Growing up, I was painfully shy. The phrase "social reject" comes to mind. To make matters worse, I hit my full height in the sixth grade. Five-foot-ten is not a popular height for a sixth-grade girl. The fact that I had a great jump shot didn't translate well socially. The guys were my best friends—but not my dates. Besides that, I was a Mormon in a very non-Mormon community. And I was a farm girl. Though our little town had all of four thousand residents, there was a clear social distinction between the town kids and the country kids. I laugh about this now, but it wasn't very funny then. There was nothing cool about being a tall, sturdy (as Grandma used to call me), Mormon farm girl. I couldn't do what my friends did, drink what they drank, or go where they went. I was different, and for a teenager, different can seem deadly.

The summer after my sophomore year I had an experience that convinced me I was destined to a life of mediocrity. Our small MIA group went to BYU Education Week, and one of the classes I attended was on the dreaded topic of self-esteem. One day, mid-lecture, the presenter suddenly pointed at me and asked me to stand and introduce myself. I was able to collect enough composure to stand, but that was about it. From there, I could manage little more than mumbling my name and slumping back down in my chair. It was pathetic.

I had obviously not demonstrated what the speaker was hoping for, so she pointed to another young woman in the audience—a tall, thin girl with beautiful, long hair. Poise oozed out of her voice and posture as she stood and introduced herself, concluding with a gracious word of thanks to the speaker for her presentation. All the while I was thinking, "Oh, sit down. She didn't ask for a eulogy." But the comparison between the two of us wasn't lost on me. Then, perhaps without realizing what she was doing, the lecturer added insult to injury when she said, "It seems that the young girl from Kansas doesn't feel as good about herself as the girl from Salt Lake City."

I was crushed. I moped in the back seat of the car all the way back to Kansas. In between little bursts of tears, I contemplated the future, and things didn't look promising. I didn't measure up, and I feared that I never would. Now, at the risk of overstating things, let me say that I had great experiences growing up, and I had disappointing experiences—just like you. But I have suffered for as long as I can remember with a deep feeling of inadequacy.

My insecurities followed me to college at BYU, and as a result I suffered socially, scholastically, and spiritually. When, during graduate school, a friendship ended in a disappointing way, I hopped in my little Toyota and drove home for a few days of consolation. For several days I moped around the house feeling sorry for myself. Then one afternoon I walked down to my brother's room and noticed his journal on his nightstand. Brad was thirteen, and I thought it might be fun to see what pearls of wisdom had fallen from the pen of my adolescent brother. The entries were predictable—about sports and girls and motorcycles. But then I came to the entry he had made the day I arrived home unexpectedly from BYU: "Sheri came home from BYU today. I'm so glad she's home. But she doesn't seem very happy. I wish there was something I could do to help her, because I really love her."

Tears began to flow. But the sweet emotions unleashed by

my brother's words triggered an even more powerful sensation. Almost instantly I had a profound feeling of divine love and acceptance wash over me and, simultaneously, a very clear impression that I ought to quit focusing on everything I didn't have, because I had enough, and it was past time to start doing something with what I did have.

For me, it was a profound moment. I didn't pop up and suddenly feel confident about life, but I couldn't deny that the Spirit had spoken and that the Lord loved me and felt I had something to contribute. It was the beginning of seeing myself with new eyes.

Now let's fast-forward a decade to my early thirties when I faced a personal disappointment involving the prospects of marriage that broke my heart. From a point of view distorted by emotional pain, I couldn't believe that anything or anyone could take away such acute loneliness or that I would ever feel happy again. In an effort to find peace, comfort, and strength, I turned to the Lord in a way I had not before. The scriptures became a lifeline, filled as they were with promises I had never noticed in quite the same way—that He would heal my broken heart and take away my pain, that He would succor me and deliver me from disappointment.

Fasting and prayer took on new intensity, and the temple became a place of refuge and revelation. What I learned was not only that the Lord could help me but that he would. Me. A regular, garden-variety, farm-grown member of the Church with no fancy titles or spectacular callings. It was during that agonizing period that I began to discover how magnificent, penetrating, and personal the power of the Atonement is. I came to sense, for perhaps the first time, what Elder Bruce C. Hafen meant when he taught that "the Atonement is not just for sinners" (*The Broken Heart,* 1).

I pleaded with the Lord to change my circumstances, because I knew I could never be happy until he did. Instead, he changed my heart. I asked him to take away my burden, but he strengthened me so that I could bear my burdens with ease (see Mosiah 24:15). I had always been a believer, but I'm not sure I had understood what, or Who, it was I believed in.

President George Q. Cannon described what I experienced: "No matter how serious the trial, how deep the distress, how great the affliction, [God] will never desert us. He never has, and He never will. He cannot do it. It is not His character. He is an unchangeable being; the same yesterday, the same today, and He will be the same throughout the eternal ages to come. . . . We may pass through the fiery furnace; we may pass through deep waters; but we shall not be consumed nor overwhelmed. We shall emerge from all these trials and difficulties the better and purer for them, if we only trust in our God and keep His commandments" ("Freedom of the Saints," 2:185).

It is tragic when we refuse to turn to Him who paid the ultimate price and to let Him lift us up. *Life is a test.* But it is only a test. A welcome and necessary test, as Brigham Young indicated when he said, "You cannot give any persons their exaltation, unless they know what evil is, what sin, sorrow, and misery are, for no person could comprehend, appreciate, and enjoy an exaltation upon any other principle" (*Journal of Discourses,* 3:369). Or, as Lehi told Jacob, his first-born in the "days of [his] tribulation in the wilderness" (2 Nephi 2:1), "it must needs be, that there is an opposition in all things. If not so, . . . righteousness could not be brought to pass, neither wickedness, neither holiness nor misery, neither good nor bad. Wherefore, all things must needs be a compound in one" (2 Nephi 2:11).

Clearly, as the Prophet Joseph received through revelation, "it must needs be that the devil should tempt the children of men, or they could not be agents unto themselves" (D&C 29:39). Thankfully, divine assistance is available to help us successfully complete this school of experience, this most critical examination called mortality.

Since that difficult period more than a decade ago, I have had many opportunities to experience the workings of the Lord in my life. He hasn't always given me what I've asked, and the answers haven't always come easily. But He has never left me alone, and He has never let me down.

Each experience with the Savior leads to greater faith, and as our faith increases, our vision of and confidence about who we are grows clearer. The more we visualize and sense through the impressions of the Spirit our ultimate potential, the more determined we become to achieve it. It's the difference between your mother hounding you to practice the piano and reaching the point where you want to do it yourself. You simply will not be denied the ultimate reward and the joy of the Big Finish.

Why is it vital that we as Latter-day Saint women have a clear vision of who we are and what we are about and have a bedrock faith in the Lord Jesus Christ? Sister Patricia Holland made a statement that is nothing short of profound: "If I were Satan and wanted to destroy a society, I think I would stage a full-blown blitz on its women" (*A Quiet Heart*, 43).

Is that not exactly what the adversary has done? Hasn't he

tried to discourage and distract us in every conceivable way? Doesn't he try to block our understanding of how spiritually sensitive our natures are, how anxious and willing the Lord is to speak to us, and how vital we are to the plan and purposes of the Lord? Satan wants us neutralized because he knows that the influence of a righteous woman can span generations.

His stated purposes are clear: He desires to make us miserable like unto himself (see 2 Nephi 2:27). He wants us to fail the test—to give up any hope of the Big Finish. Peter delivered a no-nonsense warning: "Be sober, be vigilant; because your adversary the devil, as a roaring lion, walketh about, seeking whom he may devour" (1 Peter 5:8). Indeed, through eons of practice the adversary has perfected the arts of deception, deceit, despair, and discouragement—all of which may *devour* us if we aren't constantly on the alert.

Many of Lucifer's tactics are bold and brazen and played out daily on everything from the Internet to the nightly news. But despite the fact that his handiwork is outrageously displayed at every turn—pornography, abuse, addiction, dishonesty, violence, and immorality of every kind—many of his strategies are brilliant for their subtlety. "And others will he pacify, and lull them away into carnal security, that they will say: All is well in Zion; yea, Zion prospereth, all is well—and thus the devil cheateth their souls, and leadeth them away carefully down to hell" (2 Nephi 28:21). C. S. Lewis said something similar: "The safest road to Hell is the gradual one—the gentle slope, soft underfoot, without sudden turnings, without milestones, without signposts" (*The Screwtape Letters*, 56).

There are so many loud voices in the world today, and most

of them are wrong. Most of them are trying to get our money or our support or our time or our vote or even our virtue. Many are trying to get us hooked on something. Most of them could care less about what is good for us or what will really make us happy. And many, if not most, of them—both blatant and subtle—are inspired by the adversary.

See if any of the following techniques sound familiar.

1. Satan tries to blur our vision of why we're here and to get us preoccupied with this life. He would have us distracted by and involved in anything and everything except what we came for.

2. The adversary tells us that it doesn't matter what we do now because there's plenty of time to pull our spiritual lives together later. It's the Sin Now, Repent Later Plan. He makes no mention of the ways sin corrupts our spirits and drives away *the* Spirit.

3. He feeds our vanity with promises of popularity, power, and prosperity, and tries to seduce us into believing they are the only true measure of greatness—with the hope that we will be perpetually in hot pursuit of these rewards rather than those our Father has offered us. Nephi, on the other hand, clearly taught that these lusts of the flesh belong to the kingdom of the devil and have no place in the kingdom of God (see 1 Nephi 22:23).

4. Satan wants us to feel that we're not worth a whole lot, that no matter how hard we try, we'll never make much of a difference, never make "the grade," never really measure up. He'd like us to think that we'll never be as valuable, talented, clever, poised, spiritual, intelligent, or accomplished as our mothers or colleagues or friends or other women. He loves it when we compare ourselves with each other, realizing that in such artificial comparisons we

tend to compare our areas of weakness against others' areas of strength. The result, naturally, is that we inevitably come out on the short end of the measuring stick—a measuring stick that is flawed in every respect.

Oh, sure, our work is necessary but not very important, the adversary would have us believe. *This is a big, fat lie.* It is a diversion designed to keep us so focused on any perceived injustices that we completely overlook the opportunities and privileges that are ours, underestimate the vital nature of our contribution, and never come to understand the power we have to change lives.

The world can make us feel that we're just another number—to the IRS, to the bank, to the guy who reads the gas meter. Every time I go to New York City, though I love the pulse of that city, I am impressed with how unimpressive I am. I feel swallowed up by hundreds of skyscrapers that block the light from reaching the ground, and by a sea of black limousines carrying important people (not me, by the way) to important meetings so they can do important things—or so it seems. The sheer number of people can make you feel like a tiny, insignificant blob in a mass of humanity. And yet the Great Jehovah, the creator of worlds without number, has invited us to come unto Him one by one (see 3 Nephi 11:15). He who knows even when the sparrow falls also knows our names, our needs, and our desires.

5. Satan tries to wear us down by creating the image that there is nothing glamorous in enduring to the end. It's the very reason I learned the Big Finish first, to keep the ultimate reward in front of me so that I would keep practicing those difficult technical passages that required as much endurance as skill. I have always hated talks on enduring to the end because the very phrase

makes life seem like drudgery rather than an adventure. And yet the most haunting regret imaginable would be to pass through the veil and, with the full sweep of eternity opened before our eyes, realize that we had sold our birthright for a mess of pottage, that we had been deceived by the distractions of Satan, and that the Big Finish would never be ours.

6. He tells us what we want to hear: that life is supposed to be easy and fun, and that if we experience pain or undeserved difficulties the gospel must not be working. The adversary promotes tactics that are decidedly Laman-and-Lemuelesque. When their brother launched the ridiculous effort to build a ship in the middle of the wilderness without appropriate tools, they rebelled. Their complaint, "These many years we have suffered in the wilderness, which time we might have enjoyed our possessions and the land of our inheritance; yea, and we might have been happy" (1 Nephi 17:21), suggests that one can only be happy if everything is pleasant, comfortable, and without challenge. Satan wants us to believe that happiness is directly connected to pleasures of the flesh, and that the only true religion is that which can deliver such indulgences. And at all cost he doesn't want us to learn that joy and true happiness are connected to doing a job well, rising above our weaknesses, cultivating family and other important relationships, and so on.

7. Satan always promotes shortcuts, though there are no shortcuts to anywhere worth going.

8. The adversary encourages us to criticize, judge, and evaluate each other—a practice demeaning to both the person who judges and the one who is judged. A young woman whose marriage crumbled told me how much she loves the gospel but

how weary she is of feeling that she'll never be accepted because her life hasn't unfolded as she expected and wanted it to. We ought to give up telling each other how to live our lives. It is wonderful to talk about principles, which apply equally to each of us, but it is rarely helpful to suggest how those principles should be applied.

As an example, our prophet has spoken clearly about the importance of building strong families. That's the principle. How that is accomplished, however, will vary from family to family. We could do far more good by encouraging each other to develop our spiritual sensitivities so that we can receive inspiration about our own lives, rather than judging each other on the choices we make. The Lord, after all, is in the best position to give advice. True principles are universal; applications of principle are not.

9. Lucifer whispers that life's not fair and that if the gospel were true we would never have problems or disappointments. Bad things shouldn't happen to good members of the Church, should they? The adversary would have us believe that with baptism comes a Magic Kingdom Club-like card, and that if our lives aren't like perpetual trips to Disney World, we're getting short-changed.

The gospel isn't a guarantee against tribulation. That would be like a test with no questions. Rather, the gospel is a guide for maneuvering through the challenges of life with a sense of purpose and direction. "I feel happy," Brigham Young said. "'Mormonism' has made me all I am, and the grace, the power, and the wisdom of God will make me all that I ever will be, either in time or in eternity" (*Journal of Discourses*, 8:162). President Gordon B. Hinckley said something similar: "This . . . is what the gospel is all about—to make bad men good and good men better" (*Ensign,* November 1976, 96).

International recording superstar Gladys Knight, whose accomplishments in the world of entertainment are legendary, joined the Church some ten years after her son and daughter with their families joined. When she was asked what led her to investigate the Church, she said, referring to her children, "I just watched them and their families. I watched them change. And what I saw was so remarkable that I finally decided I had better find out for myself if what they had found was true."

10. The adversary attempts to numb us into accepting a sliding scale of morality. Sometimes rationalization overtakes even the best among us. "R-rated movies don't bother me," we sometimes hear. "I go for the story, or the music, and skip over the profanity and the sexually explicit scenes." Yet advertisers pay millions of dollars for a few seconds of airtime on the bet that through brief, repeated exposures to their products we'll be persuaded to purchase them. If sixty-second ads can influence us to spend money we don't have to buy things we don't need to impress people we don't even like, then how will minutes, hours, months, and years of watching infidelity, violence, and promiscuity affect us? The measuring standard for entertainment of any kind is simple: Can you watch or participate in it and still have the Spirit with you?

I grew up watching shows such as *The Dick Van Dyke Show,* in which the lead characters, a husband and wife, slept in separate, twin beds. Contrast such restraint with the fare now offered up twenty-four hours a day on countless television stations and an endless number of Internet sites, where sexual relations are demeaned, portrayed, and glamorized. If what we see on prime time, network television had been aired back in 1971, the year I graduated from high school, there would have been a public outcry. No doubt a majority of the population would have recognized much of today's progamming as pornographic and salacious. But little by little our values have eroded and our tolerance for blatant evil has increased—such that far too often we plant our children in front of those programs and then wonder why they don't have a respect for intimacy, why they have a misguided view of marital relations, and why they question and sometimes forsake gospel standards.

11. The adversary promotes feelings of guilt—about anything. Pick a topic. You can feel guilty for having a large family. (How can any one woman possibly care for eight or nine children?) Or for having no children at all. (You are not doing your duty). For working outside the home. (Don't you know what the prophet has said about mothers who seek employment?) Or for choosing to stay home. (What's the matter, don't you have any ambition, skill, or talent?)

In some instances, guilt can be a positive emotion, for guilt is essential to true repentance. But the Savior uses other ways to help us change, often inviting us to step to a higher way of living and a more ennobling way of thinking, to do a little better and perhaps a little more. Promptings that come from Him are hopeful—even when such promptings encourage us to change, to repent, and to throw away old behaviors—and motivating rather than defeating or discouraging.

12. Lucifer works hard to undermine our innate tendency to nurture and care for others. He wants us to become separated from each other. Voice messaging and pagers are efficient, but they

don't replace a listening ear and a caring heart. If the adversary can cause us to focus more on our differences than on our similarities, if he can keep us so busy running from one commitment to another that we no longer have time for each other, he has made great strides toward neutralizing the strength and influence that we have.

We need each other. We need each other's testimonies and strength, each other's confidence and support, understanding and compassion. It is as Martin Luther said: "The kingdom of God is like a besieged city surrounded on all sides by death. Each man [and woman] has [a] place on the wall to defend and no one can stand where another stands, but nothing prevents us from calling encouragement to one another" (quoted in Jeffrey R. Holland and Patricia T. Holland, "Considering Covenants: Women, Men, Perspective, Promises," 105).

13. The father of lies rejoices in even small breaches in our integrity, because he knows that, if left unchecked, they will ultimately lead us "away *carefully* down to hell" (2 Nephi 28:21; emphasis added). Blatant sin is almost always preceded by dishonesty in one form or another.

14. The adversary would have us hung up on perfection and stymied by the commandment to become perfect. He wants this glorious potential to loom as a giant stumbling block rather than the promise of what is ultimately possible—in other words, to make the Big Finish seem little more than a dream. We should expect not to achieve perfection in this lifetime. The goal instead is to become pure, so that we are increasingly receptive to impressions inspired by the Holy Ghost.

C. S. Lewis said it this way: "Make no mistake [Christ

would say], if you let Me, I will make you perfect. The moment you put yourself in my hands, that is what you are in for. Nothing less, or other, than that. You have free will, and if you choose, you can push Me away. But if you do not push Me away, understand that I am going to see this job through. Whatever suffering it may cost you in your earthly life, . . . whatever it costs Me, I will never rest, nor let you rest, until you are literally perfect. . . . This I can do and will do. But I will not do anything less. God's demand for perfection need not discourage you in the least in your present attempts to be good, or even in your present failures. Each time you fall He will pick you up again. And He knows perfectly well that your own efforts are never going to bring you anywhere near perfection. On the other hand, you must realize from the onset that the goal towards which He is beginning to guide you is absolute perfection; and no power in the whole universe, except you yourself can prevent Him from taking you to that goal" (*Mere Christianity*, 174).

C. S. Lewis said in essence what a friend of mine described while serving a mission in Italy. At the time he wrote this letter, he had not yet seen a baptism. In that context, he wrote this: "Before my mission I thought I had a testimony, but truly it was just a weak one. I have seen the Master take my life and begin to sculpt, form, and design it. It has been amazing! At times it hasn't been easy, to say the least. I have had to succumb to His will. I know that all the sculpting, forming, and designing are not finished and that the Lord has just begun. It will take more than a lifetime to get a finished product. But it will be worth it."

It will be worth it because, if we will let Him, the Lord will change our lives. Thus, He doesn't want us to be paralyzed by our errors but to learn and grow from them. He sees us as works in progress. The faith of the brother of Jared was so strong that he was allowed to behold the Lord (see Ether 3:13). Yet prior to that remarkable event, there was a time when the Lord chastened him for three hours in a cloud (see Ether 2:14). If the scriptural account had ended there, minus "the rest of the story," our impression of this righteous man would be different. The rest of *our* stories remains to be told. It is purity, rather than perfection, that we are seeking at this stage of our eternal quest.

15. Lucifer would have us so busy—with the details swirling around family, friends, careers, and every soccer league in town—that there's no time to actually *live* the gospel. No time to fast and pray, to immerse ourselves in the scriptures, to worship in the temple—all the things we need to do to "study" for our mortal test. In other words, he wants us to be a little more concerned with the world than with the gospel, a little more interested in life today than in life forever. Regret is what happens when we figure out too late what was really important.

16. He wants us to rely on others for spiritual strength—on husbands, priesthood leaders, friends, anyone but ourselves. He loves it when we don't develop our own spiritual sensitivities and skills. He doesn't want us to learn how to get answers to prayer, or how to hear the voice of the Spirit, or how to part the veil and open up the heavens in the temple, or how to draw upon the power that comes from fasting, or how often the scriptures help prompt personal revelation. The adversary knows, and knows well, how superb the spiritual instincts are of covenanted women whose eyes are focused on the Savior, and at all cost he will try to derail and discourage us.

17. He delights in portraying religion as something restrictive and austere rather than liberating and life-giving. He wants us to know just enough about the gospel to focus on the rules and regulations rather than come to understand the joy that comes from following Christ. He depicts the Father and the Son as aloof rulers rather than our deified Father and Elder Brother Who love us, Who have a vested interest in our future, and Whose motive is to help see us through this life so that we are worthy to return to Them. He paints eternal life as something out of reach, even otherworldly, something for prophets and a few other select people, a condition you and I could never hope to achieve. And he does everything he can to block the memory of our former home.

He loves it when we seek for security in bank accounts, social status, or professional credentials when ultimate security and peace of mind come only from a connection with the Lord Jesus Christ. In short, he tries to keep us distanced from Jesus Christ. Oh fine, if we profess Him to be the Savior—talk is cheap! And if the adversary can keep us so distracted that we never really seek, embrace, and commit ourselves to the Lord, then we will also never discover the healing, strengthening, comforting power available because of the Atonement. We will never know that because of the Savior we have access to everything we need to pass this test.

The antidote to the distractions of the adversary is Jesus Christ. The Savior illuminates our vision of who we are and why we are here and gives us courage to move forward in the journey toward our heavenly home. The potential reward is a Big Finish that makes Rachmaninoff pale by comparison.

Just as Satan's motives have been clearly identified, so are the

Savior's, whose express work and glory is to "bring to pass the immortality and eternal life of man" (Moses 1:39). "He doeth not anything save it be for the benefit of the world; for he loveth the world, even that he layeth down his own life that he may draw all men unto him" (2 Nephi 26:24). The contrast between the Savior and Satan is stunning. It is the quintessential difference between light and dark, humility and arrogance, charity and self-interest, power used to bless and power used to destroy. It is the battle between good and evil personified.

A journalist stationed in Europe for the *Saturday Evening Post* during the 1930s as Hitler rose to power said this during an address at a convention in Toronto on May 2, 1941: "Before this epoch is over, every living human [will have to make a choice]. Every living human being will have lined up with Hitler or against him. Every living human being will either have opposed this onslaught or supported it. For if he tries to make no choice, that in itself will be a choice. If he takes no side, He is on Hitler's side. If he does not act, that is an act—for Hitler" *(In Our Own Words,* 130).

Is it not likewise true that before this epoch, meaning this mortal experience, is over, every living human will have to make a choice and line up either with Satan or against him? Every one of us will have either opposed Satan's onslaught or supported it. And if we attempt to make no choice, that in itself will be a choice. For if we take no side, we will be, in essence, on Satan's side. If we do not act for the Lord, we are indeed acting in behalf of the adversary.

More than a decade ago, President Ezra Taft Benson issued this charge: "There has never been more expected of the faithful in such a short period of time than there is of us. Never before on the face of this earth have the forces of evil and the forces of good been as well organized. . . . The final outcome is certain—the forces of righteousness will win. But what remains to be seen is *where* each of us . . . will stand in the battle—and *how tall* we will stand. . . . Great battles can make great heroes and heroines" ("In His Steps," 8 February 1987).

More than ever before, the Lord needs our faith and faithfulness, our vitality and ingenuity, our unwavering commitment and conviction. We are witnesses of the Lord Jesus Christ, the living capstone of all that has come before us and a vital link to all that lies ahead.

This life is a test. It is also a glorious privilege.

CHAPTER 6

WE ARE NOT ALONE

THE CHALLENGES OF LIFE NOTWITHSTANDING, WE
HAVE NOTHING TO FEAR. FOR THOSE WHO HAVE
BEEN GIVEN THE UNSPEAKABLE GIFT OF THE HOLY
GHOST NEED NEVER FEEL ALONE.

I T HAS BEEN NEARLY THREE YEARS since I received one of
those dreaded early-morning phone calls. My younger
brother Steve, who was just thirty-nine, had suffered a mas-
sive heart attack and died during the night. In an instant, and
without warning, my brother—and my most trusted friend—was
gone.

During the next few days many who loved Steve and his
wife and children traveled to their home in Colorado. But it wasn't
until *after* the funeral, when our family greeted friends who gathered at the cemetery, that I realized that seven dear friends of
mine had made the long trip from Salt Lake City to attend the
service. What made their attendance all the more remarkable was
that not one of them had ever met my brother. They had come to
support me. You can imagine my emotions as they encircled me
and said, "We just didn't want you to be alone today." In word and
deed, they taught a divine principle: It is not good, nor is it
intended, for any of us to be alone.

The pain and pangs of loneliness of one kind or another seem to be part of the mortal experience and of the process leading to sanctification. But the Lord in His mercy has made it so that we need never deal with the challenges of mortality alone.

I was thinking about this on one occasion as I sat through a meeting where the speaker seemed preoccupied with focusing on "how *hard* it is to live the gospel." By the end of the meeting, I felt depressed. He had made living the gospel seem like a sentence to life on the rock pile. As I thought later about why that message was so unsettling to me, I realized that it was because he had put the emphasis in exactly the wrong place—a common mistake, by the way. It's not living the gospel that's hard. It's *life* that's hard. It's picking up the pieces when covenants have been compromised or values violated that's hard. The gospel is the Good News that provides us with the tools to cope with the mistakes and miscalculations, the heartaches and heartbreaks, the pressures and disappointments we can expect to experience here in mortality.

How often do we make the mistake of talking to our youth and to each other about how hard it is to do everything that's expected of us, how difficult it is to maintain self-control and resist the enticements of the world? Shouldn't we instead be focusing on the doctrine of joy wrapped up in the gospel of Jesus Christ?

When Joseph Smith was asked how the Church differed from other religions of the day, he responded that the distinction lay in the gift of the Holy Ghost and that "all other considerations were contained in [that] gift" (*History of the Church*, 4:42). It therefore should behoove all those who are serious about being followers of Christ to pray for the influence and guidance of the Holy Ghost as the heavenly gift we most desire.

Nephi taught that those who receive the Holy Ghost may "speak with the tongue of angels" (2 Nephi 32:2), and that the Holy Ghost will show its recipients "all things what [they] should do" (2 Nephi 32:5). Consider for a moment the extent and impact of such a promise: that if we truly *receive* the Holy Ghost—which could be interpreted to mean not only receiving the ordinance but receiving the gift by striving to live worthy of it—we may have the companionship of a member of the Godhead. What a transcendent privilege and promise!

On one occasion Brigham Young was asked how he guided his people by revelation. He answered: "I teach them to live so that the Spirit of revelation may make plain to them their duty day by day that they are able to guide themselves. To get this revelation it is necessary that the people live so that their spirits are as pure and clean as a piece of blank paper that lies on the desk before the inditer, ready to receive any mark the writer may make upon it" (*Journal of Discourses,* 11:241).

On another occasion he taught: "Take a course to open and keep open a communication with your Elder Brother or file leader—our Saviour. Were I to draw a distinction in all the duties that are required of the children of men, from first to last, I would place first and foremost the duty of seeking unto the Lord our God until we open the path of communication from heaven to earth—from God to our own souls. Keep every avenue of your hearts clean and pure before him" (*Journal of Discourses,* 8:339).

President John Taylor was also abundantly clear about the properties and the necessity of the Spirit. "I do not care how learned a man may be, or how extensively he may have traveled," he said. "I do not care what his talent, intellect, or genius may be, at what college he may have studied, how comprehensive his views or what his judgment may be on other matters, he cannot understand certain things without the Spirit of God, and that necessarily introduces . . . the necessity of revelation. Not revelation in former times, but present and immediate revelation, which shall lead and guide those who possess it in all the paths of life here, and to eternal life hereafter" (*The Gospel Kingdom*, 35).

Lorenzo Snow said that it is the "grand privilege of every Latter-day Saint . . . to have the manifestations of the spirit every day of our lives . . . [so] that we may know the light, and not be groveling continually in the dark" (in Conference Report, April 1899, 52). And his sister Eliza, who was present at the founding of the Relief Society and served as its second general president, said this about the gift of the Holy Ghost: "When you are filled with the Spirit of God, and the Holy Ghost rests upon you . . . do you have any trials? I do not think you do. For that satisfies and fills up every longing of the human heart, and fills up every vacuum. When I am filled with that spirit my soul is satisfied; and I can say, in good earnest, that the trifling things of the day do not seem to stand in my way at all. But just let me loose my hold of that spirit and power of the Gospel, and partake of the spirit of the world, in the slightest degree, and trouble comes; there is something wrong. I am tried; and what will comfort me? You cannot impart comfort to me that will satisfy." Thus, she concludes, "Is it not our privilege to so live that we can have this constantly flowing into our souls?" (*Woman's Exponent*, 15 September 1873, 63).

In the same address Eliza declared: "You may talk to the

[Saints] about the follies of the world . . . till dooms day, and it will make no impression. But . . . place them in a position where they will get the Holy Ghost, and that will be a sure protection against outside influences."

In short, we have been promised the constant companionship of the third member of the Godhead and hence the privilege of receiving revelation for our own lives. We are not alone!

The Holy Ghost enlarges our minds, our hearts, and our understanding; helps us subdue weaknesses and resist temptation; inspires humility and repentance; guides and protects us in miraculous ways; and gifts us with wisdom, divine encouragement, peace of mind, patience, a desire to change, and the ability to differentiate between the philosophies of men and revealed truth. The Holy Ghost is the minister and messenger of the Father and the Son, and He testifies of both Their glorious, global reality and Their connection to us personally. Without the presence of the Spirit, it is impossible to comprehend our personal mission or to have the reassurance that our course is right. It is impossible to detect the subtleties and avoid the distractions and deceptions of the adversary. No mortal comfort can duplicate that of the Comforter.

Is it any wonder, then, that President Gordon B. Hinckley has said: "There is no greater blessing that can come into our lives than . . . the companionship of the Holy Spirit" (Boston Massachusetts Regional Conference, 22 April 1995).

The Lord places no limits on our access to Him. But we, unfortunately, often do. We limit ourselves when we sin; when we are lazy spiritually; when we get so busy that we are doing little more than going through one frenetic, frenzied day after another; when we fail to ask and seek.

The sixth section of the Doctrine and Covenants is a rich tutorial about our accessibility to the Spirit. In it, we are told that if we ask, we will receive; that if we inquire, the mysteries of God will be unfolded to us; and that if we build our lives upon the rock of Jesus Christ, neither earth nor hell will prevail against us. In the Sermon on the Mount the Savior promised that "*every one* that asketh receiveth; and he that seeketh findeth" (Matthew 7:8; emphasis added). He didn't say just the adorable ones, or the cute ones, or the really smart ones, or those with two or more children. He said *every one* who seeks and asks.

The best way I know to strengthen our personal testimonies and protect ourselves from evil is to seek to have as many experiences with the Lord as possible. When Satan tempted Moses, he rejected him outright, saying, "I will not cease to call upon God, . . . for his glory has been upon me, wherefore I can judge between him and thee" (Moses 1:18). Moses resisted the master of evil by relying upon previous experience with God, which had taught him to discern good from evil and to treasure the fruits of the Spirit.

There is *nothing* as exhilarating as the Spirit, and those most susceptible to Satan are those who haven't tasted of its sweetness, who do not hearken to its promptings, and who are left to deal with life alone.

This Church is a church of revelation. Our challenge is not one of getting the Lord to speak to us. Our challenge is hearing what He has to say. He has promised, "As often as thou hast inquired thou hast received instruction of my Spirit" (D&C 6:14).

Remember young Samuel, who lived with the priest Eli? One night the Lord called Samuel's name. Thinking it was Eli, Samuel ran to Eli's room. This happened three times before Eli realized and explained to his young charge Who was calling. When the Lord called again, Samuel was able to recognize the voice and respond: "Speak; for thy servant heareth" (1 Samuel 3:10). In order for us to say, "Speak; for thy servant heareth," we've got to be able to hear what the Lord, through the Spirit, has to say.

Learning to hear the voice of the Lord is like learning a language, the language of revelation. Learning any language takes time. It takes repetition and practice. It takes an immersion in that language. And it takes learning the rules that govern the language. If we were learning Portuguese or Chinese, we would not only have to memorize vocabulary words but learn syntax and grammar as well. Similarly, as we set out to better learn the language of revelation, there are guidelines and rules to govern us.

The rules of the language of revelation are found in the scriptures, which teach that we are the ones who initiate personal revelation. We do so first by having faith or believing that the Lord will respond when we ask. Sometimes we must ask many times, over a period of time, before certain answers become clear. But if we ask, we will receive (see D&C 6:5).

Thus, if you still wonder what the Spirit feels like or "sounds" like in your heart and mind, ask. As you begin to pray, *ask* if the Holy Ghost will come and be with you. Ask to learn what it feels like when He does. Ask if the Lord will help you understand, little by little as you work and pray, to better recognize His promptings and whisperings. Ask.

Remember what Alma taught? That we should "cry unto God for *all* [our] support." That *all of our doings* should be unto the Lord. That whithersoever we go, it should be unto the Lord. That *all our thoughts* should be directed to him, and that we may counsel with Him in all our doings (see Alma 37:36–37). We cannot comprehend the extent of the Lord's interest in us, and the reach of His mercy. But as remarkable as it may seem, He has issued an open invitation: "Ye are commanded in *all things* to ask of God, who giveth liberally" (D&C 46:7; emphasis added). Notice, He didn't say, "Ask me about the top items on your list, and perhaps, just maybe, I'll respond." He said, "Ask me about everything, and I will respond freely and generously." But it all begins when we ask.

The scriptures also teach that there are other things we can do to improve the line of communication between ourselves and the Lord. These include fasting and praying, which invite the spirit of revelation (see Alma 17:3); worshiping in the temple, where we are "prepared to obtain every needful thing" (D&C 109:15); immersing ourselves in the scriptures, which are a Liahona-like conduit for personal revelation; both forgiving and seeking forgiveness; and repenting regularly, which is the key to increasing personal purity and therefore receptiveness to the promptings of the Holy Ghost. Repentance increases our desire to be obedient, and our obedience is fundamental to hearing the voice of the Lord.

These are just a few of the "rules" governing the language of revelation. Indeed, the promises the Lord makes to us are stunning in this regard: "To them will I reveal all mysteries, yea, all the hidden mysteries of my kingdom. . . . Yea, even the wonders of eternity shall they know, . . . and their wisdom shall be great, and their understanding reach to heaven; . . . For by my Spirit will I enlighten them, and by my power will I make known unto them the secrets of my will" (D&C 76:7–10).

Consider just a few of the gifts we receive from the Holy Ghost. First and foremost, the Holy Ghost testifies of Christ. The presence of this gift is foundational to our faith, for our testimonies begin and are subsequently enlarged by witnesses of the Spirit that Jesus is the Christ. The Holy Ghost also helps us acknowledge and overcome our weakness (see Ether 12:27); prompts us to repent (see Moses 5:14); teaches us all things (see John 14:26); inspires charity and love; prompts, warns, and guides us (see D&C 8:2–4); helps us forgive—ourselves as well as others; heals relationships and tempers emotions; warns and guides us; helps us comprehend things we will never understand on our own; increases discernment and enables us to receive personal revelation (see D&C 11:13–14); inspires tenderness and humility; strengthens us during trials and brings comfort and peace; enhances any natural abilities we have; helps us obey; enlightens our minds and fills our souls with joy (see D&C 11:13); enables us to teach and testify (see 2 Nephi 33:1); helps us detect deception and identify truth; and even makes us more beautiful, as Parley P. Pratt suggested (see *Key to the Science of Theology*, 61). (That last one alone ought to catch our attention.)

If we hope to avoid the distractions and deceptions of the adversary; if we hope to feel peace even when life's circumstances are troubling; if we hope to have divine direction for our lives, it is vital that we learn to hear the voice of the Lord. Yet too often we fail to seek and ask. Perhaps we don't know how and haven't made it a priority to learn. Or we're so aware of our personal failings that we don't feel worthy, don't really believe the Lord will talk to us, and therefore don't seek revelation. Or perhaps we've allowed the distractions and pace of our lives to crowd out the

Spirit. What a tragedy! For the Holy Ghost blesses us with optimism and wisdom at times of challenge that we simply cannot muster on our own. No wonder one of the adversary's favorite tactics is busyness—getting us so preoccupied with the flurry of daily life that we fail to immerse ourselves in the gospel of Jesus Christ.

But we simply can't afford not to seek the things of the Spirit. There is too much at stake. Too many people are depending on us as parents and siblings, leaders and friends. A person led by the Lord knows where to turn for answers and for peace. Such people can make difficult decisions and face problems with confidence because they take their counsel from the Spirit and from their leaders who are also guided by the Spirit.

One day while reading about Nephi's instructions to build a ship, I found myself thinking, But *how* did Nephi understand so clearly what the Lord was telling him? That question launched me on a search for every scriptural evidence I could find of direct communication between God and man. At each one I made a little red *x* in the margin of my scriptures. Now, many years later, my scriptures are littered with little red *x*s, each an indication that the Lord does indeed communicate with His people. At least one crucial reason we have been admonished to immerse ourselves in the Book of Mormon and other latter-day scripture is that these holy books are filled with evidences of the Lord's willingness to communicate with His children.

I have experienced this for myself. I remember a time when a personal disappointment left me exquisitely lonely. One day while searching the scriptures for consolation, I had the impression that I needed to focus on one particular verse—a verse that I had read countless times but that suddenly revealed a depth of dimensions I had never considered before. That verse led me to literally hundreds of others in what became a period of intense searching. But it wasn't until three years later that another passage leaped out at me as if in neon. Only then was I given to understand what the Lord had been trying to teach me all that time about the power of the Atonement to ease our burdens. Some of the clearest promptings I have ever received have come while I was immersed in the scriptures. They are a conduit for revelation. They teach us the language of the Spirit.

Our ability to hear spiritually is linked to our willingness to work at it. President Hinckley has often said that the only way he knows to get anything done is to get on his knees and plead for help and then get on his feet and go to work. That combination of faith and hard work is the consummate curriculum for learning the language of the Spirit. The Savior taught, "Blessed are all they who do *hunger* and *thirst* after righteousness, for they shall be filled with the Holy Ghost" (3 Nephi 12:6; emphasis added). Hungering and thirsting translate to sheer spiritual labor.

Elder Bruce R. McConkie said, "There is no price too high, . . . no sacrifice too great, if out of it all we . . . enjoy the gift of the Holy Ghost" (*A New Witness for the Articles of Faith,* 253). What are we willing to do, what weaknesses and indulgences will we give up, to have as our personal protector and guide the constant companionship of the Holy Ghost?

It is a question worth asking, for there is a truth about which we ought to be very clear: The adversary will do anything to separate us from the Spirit. Lucifer wants us to feel alone and isolated. He wants us to try to live drawing solely upon our own genius and without the influence of the heavens, because he knows that we will never do as well or feel as well on our own as we do when we have the Spirit to guide us, strengthen us, protect us, and soothe us. And if he can keep us off balance, never really realizing our potential or capacity, he can undermine our progression and the welfare of our families as well as the entire Church.

In the spring of 1998 I spent a day in Siberia. As I walked into a drab rented hall to meet with the sisters there, the Spirit overwhelmed me and turned that dreary setting into an oasis. I knew that I was in the presence of women who were beloved of the Lord—our sister pioneers in Russia. I wondered if that was what it would have felt like to be with Emma and Eliza in Nauvoo. I wasn't the only one who felt it. Near the meeting's end, Sister Efimov, the mission president's wife, leaned over and, in what few English words she knew, whispered, "Very Holy Ghost." Very Holy Ghost indeed! The Spirit simply cannot be restrained among righteous women who are doing their best.

No wonder President Joseph F. Smith said that "it is the right and privilege of every man, every woman, and every child who has reached the years of accountability, to enjoy the spirit of revelation, and to be possessed of the spirit of inspiration. . . . It is the privilege of every individual member of the Church to have revelation for his own guidance, for the direction of his life and conduct" (*Gospel Doctrine*, 34).

It is the Holy Ghost who leads us to the Lord, who binds us to Him, and who irrevocably seals our testimony of Him. Just as my friends supported me in a time of great need, so may we have the Holy Ghost to strengthen and to guide us in times of need and challenge.

We are not alone. The Lord will never forget us. He will

never leave us alone or let us down. For His promise is clear and unimpeachable: "As well might man stretch forth his puny arm to stop the Missouri river in its decreed course, or to turn it up stream, as to hinder the Almighty from pouring down knowledge from heaven upon the heads of the Latter-day Saints" (D&C 121:33).

CHAPTER 7

MEMBERSHIP
HAS ITS PRIVILEGES

BECAUSE OF OUR MEMBERSHIP IN THE LORD'S
CHURCH, WE HAVE A HOST OF MAGNIFICENT SPIRITUAL
PRIVILEGES THAT ALLOW US TO
REGULARLY COMMUNICATE WITH AND RECEIVE
ENCOURAGEMENT FROM HOME.

O NE LABOR DAY a friend asked if I would like to accompany her family on a hike of Mount Olympus, an imposing peak on the eastern rim of the Salt Lake Basin that I had always wanted to climb. "Sure," I said. It sounded like the perfect way to spend a holiday. Until, that is, we got there and I took a closer look at the height of the peak we were going to scale. It hadn't looked *that* tall from the car as I zoomed past it every day on my way to work. But my perspective changed dramatically standing at its base.

We hiked, and hiked, and hiked. Like most things in life, the *idea* of climbing a mountain and breathing in all of that great alpine air is more romantic than actually doing it. The terrain proved to be, well, a whole lot more vertical than I had bargained for, and that day the heat exacerbated the experience. After a couple of hours of escalating pain in lungs and limbs (not to mention my feet because of shoes that didn't fit properly) it dawned on me that there were better ways to spend a day off. So, in the most nonchalant tone I could muster (I had my pride to contend with, after all), I called out between huffs and puffs to my friend on the trail ahead of me, "How much farther is it? Can we see exactly where we're going yet?" She looked up at the mountain range ahead of us and pointed to a peak that didn't seem too far away. I was just beginning to think that maybe I could do it when her husband interrupted and said, pointing his index finger upward at a ninety-degree angle, "No, that's not Mount Olympus. The peak we're going to is over there."

That peak "over there" was a huge summit a long way away, and with one glimpse I was convinced there was no way I would be able to drag my body that high or far. It took only a minute for me to say, again trying to sound casual and carefree, "You know, I don't think I really want to go to the top today. I think I'll stay and explore this part of the mountain, and then meet you at the bottom later on."

My friend, who is the ultimate "never-say-die" sort of gal, didn't so much as glance back over her shoulder as she called back to me, "Oh, no you don't! You're not getting off that easily. You're going to the top. Trust me on this one. It will be worth it."

For the next few minutes I silently debated the pros and cons. Was I going to keep climbing, or was I not? No one could *make* me keep climbing, after all. But then, somehow, my sense of competition kicked in. If everyone else could do it, I could do it. I didn't want to be the only laggard.

Thankfully, I wasn't. I lost two toenails and pulled a hamstring in the process, but thanks to my friend's prodding, I made it. And she was right. Was it ever worth it! The view from the top of that jagged peak was breathtaking and more than worth the blisters and pounding lungs. As we sat at the pinnacle and watched the eagles soar *beneath* us, I thought, *I wouldn't have missed this for the world.*

But I almost did miss it—as well as some fundamental principles that the climbing of Mount Olympus reinforced firsthand:

First, when the going got hard, I was ready to give up and settle for something much less than the reward I ultimately received by reaching the top.

Second, had it not been for the encouragement from a friend who had been to the top before and knew what awaited us there, I would have stopped.

Third, there came a point where I had to decide for myself if I was going to keep going or not. All the encouragement notwithstanding, no one could force me to go to the top.

Fourth, what I found on top was more spectacular than anything I had imagined or been able to see from down below. The reward exceeded all expectations.

And fifth, to have the mountaintop experience, I had to make the climb. There was no shortcut.

That experience on the mountain is a lot like mortality. In fact, our mortal probation *is* a mountain filled with ridges and peaks and steep hikes. Sometimes, when the going gets difficult, we feel like giving up. We've perhaps all had days or moments along our mortal climb toward sanctification and ultimately eternal life when we have said to ourselves, if even momentarily, "This is too hard. I can't go another step. Whatever is up there can't possibly be worth what I am going through down here." Others—

prophets, apostles, family members, leaders, and friends—can urge us onward and help us through the discouraging times. But when it comes right down to it, we have to decide for ourselves if we are willing to make the climb.

There is no shortage of mountains to climb. And as painful and difficult as some of these tests of endurance, sheer will, and faith are, they are often the catalyst to our greater understanding. They teach us that because of the Atonement there are power, peace, comfort, healing, and strength available to help us make the climb.

Thank heavens—literally—for the magnificent gift of the Lord Jesus Christ. For we all encounter obstacles and disappointments in this life. They are part of the journey.

I laughed when I opened a greeting card that showed five dogs on the front who had cornered a cat. The front panel of the card read, "They say you learn the most from your most difficult experiences." Inside: "What a stupid system."

Challenges and trials do, however, appear to be part of the Lord's "system," for he "seeth fit to chasten his people; yea, he trieth their patience and their faith" (Mosiah 23:21). Apparently, because of our natural-man tendencies, we are responsible for bringing at least part of this on ourselves, for "except the Lord doth chasten his people with many afflictions, . . . they will not remember him" (Helaman 12:3).

What that greeting card really says is that the mortal climb is hard—harder, in fact, than anything we have experienced to this point in our eternal existence, and perhaps the most difficult period we will ever experience. Things don't always turn out as we think or hope they will. Prayers aren't always quickly and neatly answered. Children don't always obey, despite the best efforts of devoted parents. Our health doesn't always hold up, even if we live the Word of Wisdom faithfully. Money doesn't always appear when we need it, even if we're faithful to the tithe. Interactions with employers and neighbors and business associates and family members and a myriad of other circumstances aren't always fair (which is one sure sign that your individually tailored curriculum is on course). Those we love don't always love us back or honor their commitments. Loved ones die, despite prayers and pleadings for healings and protection. Marriages sometimes fail. Trusted friends and colleagues at times undermine and betray us.

We have all stood at the base of plenty of mountains. There was a time when I was working at a small company where I shouldered much of the responsibility and pressure for bringing in enough money to make payroll. I was working many more than forty hours a week, and in my spare time trying to complete a project that was in itself a major undertaking. It was during this period that my mother was diagnosed with cancer. In the middle of her chemotherapy treatments, she became deathly ill with a blood clot in her lung and had to be hospitalized. Then, while she was in the hospital recuperating from the blood clot, *her* mother passed away. I'll never forget walking into Mom's hospital room to tell her that her mother was gone. I returned to Utah to represent Mother at Grandma's funeral, and a few days later the company I was working for went out of business and I was out of a job.

I remember thinking that the solution to these problems was to never answer the phone again, as every ring seemed to bring more bad news. Then one day, in the midst of despair, I happened upon a verse of scripture that leaped off the page: "If it so be that the children of men keep the commandments of God he doth nourish them, and strengthen them, and provide means whereby they can accomplish the thing which he has commanded them" (1 Nephi 17:3). Emotionally, physically, and spiritually exhausted, I was in desperate need of nourishment and strength. That verse was like a spiritual elixir because it reminded me that I wasn't supposed to make this climb alone, that there was help from a Source far greater than anything earthly.

Since that time, there have been other mountains even steeper and more difficult to climb. But I have come to understand that the mountains—meaning challenges and obstacles—are designed to help lead us ultimately to the Mount—meaning the Mount of the Lord—where there awaits more than we can possibly imagine from here below.

One sister who crossed the plains with the early pioneers described the process well in her journal: "It wouldn't be bad to walk fifteen hundred miles if one had a feather-bed to sleep on at night. But no matter how I folded it, it was too bulky. When it came to choosing between Zion and a feather-bed, well, it was a little too late to turn my back on Zion" (quoted in Proctor, *The Gathering*, back cover).

Indeed: It is too late to turn our backs on Zion.

Moses could teach us something about getting sidetracked en route to the Mount. There he was on the mount communing with the Lord, desperately wanting his people to make the spiritual climb ahead of them and claim this reward for themselves. But instead, down below in the valley his people had already become so restless that they had molded a golden calf and proclaimed it their god. Finally the Lord instructed Moses to return to his people: "Go, get thee down; for thy people . . . have corrupted themselves: They have turned aside quickly out of the way which I commanded them" (Exodus 32:7–8).

Moses had talked with the Lord face to face. He had learned what it was to be endowed with power from on high. But the children of Israel were not willing to make the climb.

It is by climbing the spiritual mountain that we learn how to deal with the other mountains, or problems, in our lives, that we find the power and energy and insight and strength to deal with what lies along and in our path.

The question, then, is, How do we climb the spiritual mount?

Some years ago a credit card company launched a campaign designed to attract customers by appealing to the desire to become a member of an elite group entitled to special privileges. The "membership has its privileges" campaign was a clever tactic, for who doesn't appreciate privileges?

Although the privileges associated with that particular company are debatable, there is no debate that membership in The Church of Jesus Christ of Latter-day Saints does have its privileges, remarkable spiritual privileges. Consider a few of the obvious ones:

First, as stated previously, we have the Holy Ghost to guide us, bless us, protect us, and make us smarter than we are. Said President John Taylor, "Without revelation religion is a mockery and a farce. If I can not have a religion that will lead me to God, and place me *en rapport* with him, and unfold to my mind the principles of immortality and eternal life, I want nothing to do with it" (*The Gospel Kingdom,* 35). Happily, our Father has provided many ways for His children to communicate with and receive instruction from Him—beginning with the gift of the Holy Ghost.

Further, we know who we are and Whose we are. We understand why we are here and where we may ultimately go, and therefore have a sense of purpose and direction and potential. We understand the Great Plan of Redemption. We have a living prophet who provides clear, unbiased, inspired direction that we may rely on with complete confidence. We have in our midst the priesthood, which is the greatest power on earth and the only power that can and will be used only to bring about righteousness. Because of priesthood power, we may receive the gift of the Holy Ghost, participate in ordinances that bind us to each other and to the Lord, and have access to "all the spiritual blessings of the church" (D&C 107:18).

Temples where we may be endowed with power from on high and learn more about parting the veil between ourselves and the Lord now dot the earth. Modern-day scripture provides insight into the Atonement and the fulness of the gospel of Jesus Christ available nowhere else. Among other things, we know that the Lord is the "same yesterday, today, and forever," and that all the spiritual gifts of which He has ever spoken "never will be done away" (Moroni 10:19) and are therefore available to us today—the gift to behold angels, the gift to heal and be healed, the gift to "work mighty miracles" and teach the word of knowledge, the gift to speak in "divers kinds of tongues," and the gift to have "great faith" (Moroni 10:8–16).

The spiritual privileges available to us are remarkable, for they allow us to regularly communicate with and receive encouragement from home, meaning our heavenly home.

Brigham Young taught that "if the Latter-day Saints will walk up to their privileges, and exercise faith in the name of Jesus Christ, and live in the enjoyment of the fulness of the Holy Ghost constantly day by day, there is nothing on the face of the earth that they could ask for, that would not be given to them" (*Discourses of Brigham Young*, 156). What a promise!

And yet, on another occasion, he lamented: "There is no doubt, if a person lives according to the revelations given to God's people, he may have the Spirit of the Lord to signify to him His will, and to guide and to direct him in the discharge of his duties, in his temporal as well as in his spiritual exercise. I am satisfied, however, that in this respect, *we live far beneath our privileges*" (*Journal of Discourses*, 12:104; emphasis added).

One can't help but wonder how many gifts of the Spirit, how much spiritual direction, and how many spiritual privileges we haven't received because we are living beneath them—meaning that we don't have the faith to receive them, or that we aren't living worthy of them, or that we *feel* we're not worthy, or because we are lazy or inexperienced or distracted or any number of reasons that we don't actively seek after them. Once again, the sobering reality is that *we* determine how clear our communication will be, how strong our bond will be, how thin the veil will be, and how many spiritual privileges we will claim.

I am technologically impaired. I can't even make my VCR stop blinking. But I've used a computer for twenty years, and I can't imagine life without it—though frankly I know how to do only a few things well. Compared to my brother, who works in the software industry, I'm computer illiterate. He knows how to do much more than I do using the same computer and the same programs. At least a hundred times he has offered to show me how to work better and faster. But he always seems to offer when I'm facing a huge deadline and don't have time to learn to do things better and faster. (Note the irony.) I continue to just get by, doing what little I know how to do but leaving a tremendous source of power untapped.

How many of us are spiritually just getting by rather than learning how to access the divine power available to those who seek after it?

The Prophet Joseph rehearsed a vision he had where he saw nine of the Twelve serving in a foreign land, presumably England. Gathered in a circle, his brethren appeared discouraged and downtrodden. But standing above them was the Savior, who was weeping as He looked upon His servants. The Prophet's impression was that Christ wanted desperately to comfort them and lift them up, but they didn't see Him because they were looking down, not up (see *Teachings of the Prophet Joseph Smith*, 107).

The Lord told Nephi that "unto him that receiveth I will give more; and from them that shall say, We have enough, from them shall be taken away even that which they have" (2 Nephi 28:30). In this case, could the word *receive* have several meanings—to accept, to believe, to seek after? Don't we actually "receive" what the Lord has for us when we believe Him and His doctrine, and when we then seek after the gifts He has made available?

The best way I know to strengthen our personal testimonies, to draw upon the privileges available to us, and thus to protect ourselves and our families from evil, is to seek to have as many experiences with the Lord as possible. Meaningful experiences with the Lord increase (in quantity and quality) as we yield to the enticings of the Holy Spirit. Yielding to the Spirit is the only way we can hope to overcome the natural man, who wants to control, is self-indulgent and self-absorbed, rarely if ever wants what is good for him, and is impatient, egotistical, and demanding. When Jesus said, "The spirit indeed is willing, but the flesh is weak" (Matthew 26:41), he was doing more than commenting on sleepy disciples.

Yielding ourselves to the Lord always requires sacrifice and often a sacrifice of our sins. How many favorite sins are we holding on to that alienate us from the Spirit and keep us from turning our lives over to the Lord? Do we cling to things such as jealousy, or holding onto a grudge, or being casual about the Sabbath day or the way we wear the garment, or undisciplined about what we watch or read? Consider the rippling impact on our lives and our families if every one of us determined to sacrifice something that is dulling our spiritual senses!

Yielding ourselves to the Lord, from whom we may obtain greater strength than we will ever muster on our own, is the only source of strength in this life and happiness in the life to come. I think of a sister missionary who was the first young woman in her Bulgarian city to be baptized. Her family subsequently disowned her. Yet she said through her tears: "I had never heard of Jesus Christ. But when the missionaries taught me about Him, it was like hearing something I already knew. I love this gospel, and now I have a great responsibility in how I live, because Jesus Christ has changed my life."

Such change, born of faith, is just one of the privileges we may claim as followers of Christ. In the benedictory chapter of the Book of Mormon, Moroni exhorts us to not deny the gifts of God: "Remember that [Christ] is the same yesterday, today, and forever, and that all these gifts of which I have spoken, which are spiritual, never will be done away, even as long as the world shall stand, only according to the unbelief of the children of men" (Moroni 10:19). Thus, we are as entitled to the gifts of believing and healing and working miracles and beholding angels as anyone has ever been. We are as entitled to climb the spiritual mount as any people have ever been. But these gifts are necessarily activated by our faith. And it is our willingness to believe, our willingness to "experiment" upon the word (Alma 32:27) and take the Lord at His word, and especially our willingness to seek after the spiritual privileges the Lord has made available to us, that makes us equal to the climb.

As we do this, we will make Eliza R. Snow's statement a reality—that the day would come when we, the sisters of the Church, would stand "at the head of the women of the world" because we had "greater and higher privileges than any other females upon the face of the earth" (*The Evening News*, 15 January 1870).

Those greater and higher privileges are spiritual privileges available to us because of our membership in The Church of Jesus Christ of Latter-day Saints.

CHAPTER 8

PRACTICE
MAKES PERFECT

WHEN ALMA INVITED US TO EXPERIMENT UPON THE
WORD, HE WAS ENCOURAGING US TO PRACTICE—
MEANING TO PUT THE LORD TO THE TEST,
AND IN THE PROCESS TO COME TO UNDERSTAND THE
FULL MAJESTY OF HIS MERCY AND POWER.

ONE YEAR WHILE I WAS ATTENDING BYU I invited a friend to drive home with me to Kansas for Thanksgiving. As we prepared to leave, the weather forecast looked threatening—particularly through Colorado and over the Rockies—so the night before we left, my father called and told me to buy snow chains, just in case. I resisted at first; I didn't have a clue about how to put them on, even if I did need them. But Dad prevailed, and I bought the chains. As it turned out, however, the drive home was uneventful, and the shiny new chains never came out of the box.

While we were home, Dad insisted on showing my friend and me how to install the snow chains—again, just in case. Again, I resisted. I couldn't be bothered. But my friend was willing to endure Snow Chains 101, and she learned how to put them on.

That was more than good enough for me. I had made that drive a hundred times, *sans* chains, and I *knew* we wouldn't need them.

The trip back to Provo, Utah, proved to be unlike any other, however. We were barely into the Rockies when we came upon the iciest roads I had ever seen. For an hour or so we inched along, the speedometer needle scarcely registering. Finally my friend asked if we shouldn't put the chains on. But I didn't want to take the time. Surely the icy conditions wouldn't stretch much farther.

Not five minutes later we crept around a hairpin curve just in time to see a car slide off the road ahead of us and plummet into the Colorado River several hundred feet below. At that, my obstinacy having suddenly run its course, I pulled over and we began the ordeal of attempting to install the chains. *Ordeal* is not too strong a word here. The process proved aggravating beyond belief—and no doubt hilarious to anyone watching. Unfortunately, because I had paid scant attention to Dad's snow chain tutorial, it was left to my friend to patiently lead us step-by-step through the process. Ninety frozen minutes later, we finally had the "easy-install" chains in place and were back on the road. But even after all that, we had done something incorrectly, for as we headed down the road the chains clanked against the chassis with every revolution of the tires.

By now I had lost my sense of humor. And the banging chains didn't help. So you can imagine my reaction when, less than fifteen minutes later, we drove suddenly out of the ice into sunny skies and onto bare roads. Muttering that I had known all along that we didn't need to put those blasted chains on, I pulled over, removed the chains, and threw them into the trunk. We had wasted more than an hour, and for no good reason.

For several hours we drove on, attempting to make up time as we went. But we were so far behind schedule that we were still on the road late that night. Sometime past midnight we ran into a horrible blizzard halfway up the last mountain pass between us and home. Unable to see even the sides of the road, we inched along until we finally arrived at the summit, where a turnout area allowed us to pull over, along with dozens of other motorists. The snow was coming down hard and sideways, and it was bitter cold. Conditions were ten times worse than they had been when we put the chains on the first time, but we had no choice. Bracing ourselves, we hopped out, pulled the chains from the trunk, and began the ordeal all over again.

This time, however, the episode wasn't nearly as aggravating. Because we had been through the process just a few hours earlier, we had the routine down. In fact, a truck driver who had also pulled over approached us and said, "Well, I was coming over to help you girls, but it looks as though you know what you're doing," and walked off. *Chivalry is dead,* I thought.

Thankfully, in ten minutes we had the chains on and were headed back down the road—and without that telltale clanking this time. The second time around we had done a much better, quicker job.

I have thought about the "parable of the snow chains" many times. There is no way we could have installed those chains in the dark of night in a blinding blizzard with three feet of snow already on the ground if we hadn't had a practice run earlier that day.

Practice is a wonderful concept. To do *anything* well— whether it's perfecting a turnaround jump shot, mastering a

Rachmaninoff concerto, or excelling at open-heart surgery—we've got to practice.

The same is true with developing our faith, our spiritual sensitivity, our ability to hear the voice of the Lord—in other words, our spiritual skills. They require practice. Consider the interchange between David and Goliath. An adolescent boy, dwarfed by the veteran warrior Goliath, pledges to go up against him in hand-to-hand combat. David's courage may have seemed foolhardy at the time, but he knew what he was doing because he had been practicing. His confidence came from previous experience: "The Lord that delivered me out of the paw of the lion, and out of the paw of the bear, he will deliver me out of the hand of this Philistine," he explained (1 Samuel 17:37). Twice before David had done the improbable. And because of those experiences, he knew the Lord would magnify him again and enable him to subdue Goliath.

When Moses arrived at the shores of the Red Sea, leading the children of Israel with Pharaoh and his armies in hot pursuit, did he simply wave his arms and magically part the waters? Surely he wouldn't have led his people there, knowing they could have been trapped between the sea on one side and Pharaoh's army from the rear, had he not been able to discern directions from the Lord. He had already seen and worked many miracles in which the elements were controlled. So now, when the stakes were high, Moses knew what to do. He had been practicing.

Is it possible that some of Nephi's trials—retrieving the brass plates from Laban under the most threatening conditions, breaking his bow, being bound with cords and persecuted repeatedly by his older brothers—were in fact opportunities the Lord provided for Nephi to practice so that when it came time to build a ship (with no tools, no skills, no knowledge, and little help) he would have the spiritual confidence to proceed? "If God had commanded me to do all things I could do them," he responded in faith to his taunting brothers who mocked him for even thinking about building a ship (1 Nephi 17:50).

The Lord, through our individually tailored mortal tutorials, gives us opportunities to practice, rehearse, refine, and develop our spiritual skills—and in particular, to practice having and exercising faith. With that principle in mind, consider President Spencer W. Kimball's words: "We need a storage of faith that can carry [us] over the dull, the difficult, the terrifying moments, disappointments, disillusionments, and years of adversity, want, confusion, and frustration" (*Faith Precedes the Miracle*, 110–11).

How do we increase our faith and stockpile a spiritual reserve? Among other things, we practice. Like anything else, developing the spiritual skills that can be ours takes practice, repetition, experience, and sustained effort. Alma taught it this way: "Behold, if ye will awake and arouse your faculties, even to an experiment upon my words, and exercise a particle of faith, yea, even if ye can no more than desire to believe, let this desire work in you" (Alma 32:27). Alma's invitation is filled with mercy and patience. It's as though the Lord is saying, "Just experiment. Put me to the test. See if I won't do for you what I have said I will do." In other words, practice.

It is practice—practice in building our faith, practice in obtaining spiritual gifts and accessing our spiritual privileges—that *will* make us perfect.

When you face seemingly insurmountable problems, when you plead with the Lord for help with something that you can't manage on your own, when circumstances call for direction and strength from a Source greater than anything mortal, have you found yourself wondering, as I have at particularly difficult times, *I know the Lord can help me, but will He?*

These verses in the Doctrine and Covenants are reassuring: "Verily, verily, I say unto you, ye are little children [and aren't we all children spiritually?] and ye have not as yet understood how great blessings the Father hath in his own hands and prepared for you; and ye cannot bear all things now; nevertheless, be of good cheer, for I will lead you along. The kingdom is yours and the blessings thereof are yours, and the riches of eternity are yours" (D&C 78:17–18).

We *are* little children, and we have no concept of the vast store of riches, spiritual riches, the Lord has available for us. But He has promised that if we will let Him, He will lead us along— no doubt by providing opportunities for us to experiment upon His word, opportunities to practice. We can practice having greater and more complete faith in him as our Savior, our Redeemer, and our Rescuer.

Moroni recorded these transcendent words of the Lord: "My grace is sufficient for all men that humble themselves before me; for if they humble themselves before me, and have faith in me, then will I make weak things become strong unto them" (Ether 12:27). Consider the ramifications of such a promise! We are all painfully aware of our mortal weaknesses. Imagine, then, the impact of the promise that the Savior can make our weak things become strong. This doctrine is more profound than any behavior-modification course, more penetrating than any resurgent attempts at willpower.

We can either attempt to lift the burdens (and climb the mountains) of our lives alone, or we can link ourselves to and seek help from Him who wrought the Atonement expressly so that there would be Someone to whom we could turn for help and healing.

Consider the sequence of these verses from the Doctrine and Covenants: "Look unto me in every thought; doubt not, fear not," the Lord has said. "Behold the wounds which pierced my side, and also the prints of the nails in my hands and feet" (D&C 6:36–37). It is *because* the nails pierced His hands and feet, because He submitted Himself to the Father in our behalf, that we need not fear or doubt. It is because of the power and scope of the Atonement that we have access to power to help us deal with our mortal weaknesses, our fears, our anxieties, and our lack of peace. We are connected to Someone who can and will make up the difference between who we are and who we want to be, between where we are and where we want to be—if we will come unto Him.

I, like you, have been blessed with many opportunities to exercise faith in Jesus Christ, experiment upon his word, and practice what I believe. Through those experiences I have come to know that because of the phenomenal act of atonement begun in the Garden of Gethsemane and completed on the cross at Calvary, there is power, peace, comfort, healing, and strength available to help us as we attempt to negotiate life's challenges.

I think of opportunities in recent years to practice— challenges that have demanded more patience, more energy, more wisdom, more understanding than I would ever have been able to muster on my own. I have felt the sting of betrayal; I know what it is to be the subject of widespread gossip; I know the pain of being falsely accused, undermined, and misunderstood; and like you, I have found myself again and again in circumstances that boggled my mind.

But through these challenges large and small, I am learning—as you are—that the Savior truly did compensate for *all* of the difficulty, the heartache, the betrayal, the disillusionment and disappointment, and the pain we feel and face. I have learned that, in a tangible way, He would be my companion. And through it all I have found that He will never let me down or leave me alone.

In a letter to Church headquarters one sister shared feelings that perhaps you have had at some point in your life: "I believe in the Atonement. But I fear that belief, and faith in the Savior, aren't going to keep me hanging on. I am so tired and discouraged and sad. The 'reality' we hear about in the hymns and from our Sunday talks and lessons—about day dawns breaking, and all being well, and angels from the realms of glory—is not the reality of my life, and everyday reality has become a very tough thing to continuously fight against. Endurance is beginning to look like a severely overrated commodity. I just don't feel strong anymore, and I guess I'm not sure I want to keep trying so hard to be strong."

At the time she wrote this letter, this sister believed *in* the Savior but didn't really believe Him. Some time later, after she had been able to consider the Atonement and its power to help us withstand our individual crucibles, she wrote this: "The assertion that the Atonement compensates not only for our repented-of sins but will also relieve the painful experience of mortality struck me deeply. If this is true, it answers my frustration, the feeling that I can't keep getting through these life experiences on whatever internal strength my individual faith and determination have produced. The strength must come from somewhere else, a source that is not weak, does not give out, will not falter as I am doing. I am studying the suggested scriptures, fasting, praying. I am testing—and trusting—the declaration that I can find how to access these blessings of the Atonement for myself, that He really is there in that capacity, that He will not step back from us while we endure these experiences."

The difference for this sister, and the key to her change of heart, was her willingness to practice and to experiment upon the Lord's words. Although the Lord Jesus Christ won't usually take away our problems, He also won't leave us to face them alone. Said Elder Jeffrey R. Holland: "[We] fear that God in his heaven, with all of his urgent national and international, galactic and intergalactic business, is certain to be occupied with things other than your hopes and happiness. I do not know exactly how He does it, but . . . my testimony . . . is that *nothing* in this universe is more important to him than your hopes and happiness. . . . When we pass through the veil, it will be thrilling to learn how God watches over us and cares for us, how he knows our every thought. For now it is enough to know simply that he does it" ("Considering Covenants: Women, Men, Perspective, Promises," 96–97).

With each new challenge, each new opportunity to increase our faith, comes the privilege of practicing what we believe and exercising our spiritual privileges while adding to the "storage of faith" President Kimball spoke of. Just as school requirements become more challenging from grade to grade, so do the Lord's spiritual requirements of us increase as we progress, grow, and develop. The faith we have had in the past most likely will not be sufficient to sustain us in the days ahead—both because of the world's escalating depravity and because the Lord will give us opportunities to grow and progress spiritually. Each new challenge we face can result in a deeper faith in the Lord and greater confidence in the spiritual privileges that are ours. Dealing with difficult circumstances seems to prepare us to handle even more complicated opportunities for growth.

When I was asked to help prepare President Gordon B. Hinckley's biography, I was honored, but I was also overwhelmed and more than a little terrified at the prospect. I had a demanding job, was serving as a stake Relief Society president, and now was responsible for a project filled with enough pressure, stress, and workload to itself deserve full-time attention—not to mention someone with a lot more talent.

I reorganized my life to be as efficient as possible and then began working on the book, usually scheduling time in the evening after a long day at the office to research and write. But this system didn't work. There were too many interruptions in the evenings, and it was impossible for me to do the hardest work of the day—filling a blank computer screen with coherent sentences—when I was mentally spent.

About this time, my stake president informed me that both of my counselors were wanted back in their respective wards and that I needed to select two new counselors. I was disheartened. Our presidency had been together for more than three years, and at that point we worked so seamlessly together that we could finish each other's sentences. I couldn't imagine breaking in two new counselors when I was under more pressure than I had ever been.

But through prayer, I realized that the stake president was right, and I went about the process of selecting new counselors. They were called, and I was with them when they were set apart. Before we began, the first counselor in the stake presidency, who knew nothing of the extra load I was carrying, said that though there was no need to set me apart again, he wondered if it might be appropriate for the stake president to give me a blessing.

I was grateful for the suggestion and was subsequently amazed when the stake president acknowledged, during the blessing, the weighty responsibilities that had fallen upon my shoulders, and my concern about being able to handle them all. Then he spoke these words: "I bless you that your body will require less sleep, insomuch that you will not fall asleep in the many meetings you have to attend."

For several days thereafter I pondered the implications of that promise. Finally, I began to calculate just how early I would have to get up to do my writing *before* I left for work. There would be fewer interruptions, and I would be doing the hardest work of the day when I was mentally fresh. No matter how I figured the time, however, it looked as if I would have to arise at 3:00 A.M. I am an early riser, but 3:00 A.M. seemed absurd. Yet, I could not get the words of that priesthood blessing out of my mind. I kept thinking about some of the challenges I had faced and mountains I had climbed in the past and the way the Lord had shored me up, strengthened me, and made me able to do things I could never have managed on my own. Did I, or did I not, believe that He would support and sustain me again? Surely He would. But would He really help me get by with less sleep? At first, I couldn't quite imagine it.

After pondering the blessing for several days, I decided to experiment upon His words. The long story made short is that for twenty-three months, six days a week, I arose at 3:00 A.M. Did I have the physical or mental stamina, in and of myself, to do such a thing? Absolutely not. My role in this process was simply to believe that the Lord was able *and* willing to do something for me that I could not do myself.

Many times during recent years as the weight of responsibility has intensified, I have looked back longingly at that period of time and realized that it really wasn't all that difficult. But with every experience we have experimenting upon or practicing the Lord's words, the stronger grows our faith and the greater becomes our storage of faith.

The Lord will do for us exactly what He has said He will do—if we will believe in Him and seek His divine direction and intervention in our lives. Strength and power, insight and wisdom far greater than our own are available to us. It is simply not possible for the Lord to forget us. "For can a woman forget her sucking child, that she should not have compassion on the son of her womb? Yea, they may forget, yet will I not forget thee," promised the Lord, who then reminded His followers of the sobering and spiritually sensational reality of His sacrifice for us: "Behold, I have graven thee upon the palms of my hands" (1 Nephi 21:15–16).

Do you believe that the Savior will really do for you what He has said He will do? That He will give you strength and insight to deal with the challenges at hand? That He will lighten your burden and turn your weakness into strength? That He will heal your broken heart and fill you with hope? That He will renew your energy and help you forgive? That He will help you deal with disappointment and loneliness, and fill you with the sweet knowledge of how precious you are to Him? That He will help you resist your greatest temptation? That He will respond to your deepest hurt or longing and bless you with a spirit of good cheer, optimism, and faith? That He is the only source of comfort, strength, information, knowledge, and peace that will not change, will not move, will not betray you, and will never let you down?

Mahatma Gandhi said this: "God is the hardest taskmaster I have known on this earth, and he tries you through and through. And when you find that your faith is failing or your body is failing you, and you are sinking, he comes to your assistance somehow or other and proves to you that you must not lose your faith and that he is always at your beck and call. . . . So I have found. I cannot really recall a single instance when, at the eleventh hour, he has forsaken me" *(The Treasure Chest,* 86).

The Lord's exquisite sensitivity to each of us is hard to comprehend, but it exists nonetheless. In 1985 Elder M. Russell Ballard, then of the presidency of the Seventy, and Glenn L. Pace, then representing the welfare department, traveled to Ethiopia to determine how to allocate several million dollars the Church had collected in special fasts. Ethiopia was suffering a horrid drought. There had not been rain in Addis Ababa for months. Upon arriving there they found one Church member, and on Sunday the three of them met together.

They partook of the sacrament and all bore testimonies. Then Elder Ballard suggested that they kneel in prayer. About that experience he recorded: "I pronounced a blessing, a benediction upon our fast and testimony meeting, and was impressed to invoke, by the power of the Holy Priesthood and in the name of the Lord, a blessing upon the land. This certainly was not a dedicatory blessing in any way, shape, or form, since that was not my commission or responsibility, but I felt impressed . . . to plead with the Lord in His name and by the power of the priesthood to bring rain."

After the meeting the men returned to their own rooms. Elder Ballard described what then happened: "About two or three hours into the afternoon, it clouded up and rain came pouring down. As I stood on the balcony of that hotel, tears streamed down my cheeks and I found myself on my knees expressing gratitude that the Lord had acknowledged that we were in Ethiopia on this special assignment."

Just as the Lord knew that Elder Ballard and Brother Pace were in Ethiopia, He knows where we are, what our needs and concerns are, and whether or not we are striving to have faith in Him. He is eager to respond to our inquiries and to bless us with strength and inspiration. He is willing to give us as much information, wisdom, insight, spiritual power, and peace as we are ready to handle and willing to ask for.

I repeat: The Lord will never forget us. He will never leave us alone or let us down. He has offered us, through membership in His Church, magnificent spiritual blessings—the greatest of which is the knowledge that the Savior is who He says He is, and that He will do for us what He has said He will do. Therefore, "let us cheerfully do all things that lie in our power; and then may we stand still, with the utmost assurance, to see the salvation of God, and for his arm to be revealed" (D&C 123:17).

CHAPTER 9

THE MAGNIFICENT
BLESSING OF
PRIESTHOOD POWER

THE GREATEST CHAMPION OF WOMAN AND WOMAN-
HOOD IS JESUS CHRIST, WHOSE DESIGNATIONS
REGARDING PRIESTHOOD HAVE NO BEARING ON
INDIVIDUAL WORTH OR VALUE.

W HEN PRESIDENT GORDON B. HINCKLEY is interviewed by the press, it is not at all uncommon for
him to be asked questions about the women of the
Church, with those questions often posed in a manner insinuat-
ing that Latter-day Saint women are second-class citizens in the
Church, that they have no voice, and that they are generally not
valued. President Hinckley, of course, has his own unique way of
handling these kinds of questions, as he did at the National Press
Club in the spring of 2000 when he said about the sisters of the
Church, "People wonder what we do for our women. I will tell you
what we do. We get out of their way and look with wonder at
what they are accomplishing" (National Press Club Address,
8 March 2000).

I find it curious, the general attitude of disrespect among the
media regarding the Church's treatment and view of women, for I

have been unable to identify any organization of any kind any-where in the world where more women have more influence than in The Church of Jesus Christ of Latter-day Saints. Hundreds of thousands of women serving in more than 25,000 congregations in 160 nations of the world have the rights and responsibilities of presidency, and tens of thousands more are called to teach men, women, youth, and children. Where else do so many women bear such weighty responsibility and enjoy such respect and influence?

There is simply no women's group anywhere to compare with the Relief Society, which is the only organization for women that was founded by a prophet of God and thereby may justly be con-sidered the "Lord's organization for women," as President Kimball defined it (*Ensign*, March 1976, 4). And President Joseph F. Smith made this declaration, referring to the influence of the women of the Church: "It is not for you to be led by the women of the world; it is for you to lead the world and to lead especially the women of the world, in everything that is praise-worthy, everything that is God-like, everything that is uplifting and that is purifying to the children of men" (minutes of the General Board of the Relief Society, 17 March 1914, 54). The Relief Society's purpose is to help sisters and their families come unto Christ—meaning to help women and their families grow spiritually and temporally.

Though the Prophet Joseph organized the Relief Society "after the pattern of the priesthood" and stated that the Church "was never perfectly organized until the women were thus organ-ized" (*Woman's Exponent*, 1 September 1883, 51), there are some who cite the fact that women are not ordained to the priesthood as evidence that our work and thus our influence is less significant than that of men. But such a view of the Lord's plan is incomplete and narrow, for there is no theology that embraces a more ennobling doctrine regarding women than does the restored gospel of Jesus Christ. Said Elder Bruce R. McConkie, "In all matters that pertain to godliness and holiness and which are brought to pass as a result of personal righteousness . . . men and women stand in a position of absolute equality before the Lord" (*Ensign*, January 1979, 61). And President Gordon B. Hinckley said, speaking to the sisters of the Church: "You are an essential part of [the Church], a most important part of it. It could not function properly without you. You provide inspiration. You provide balance. You constitute a vast reservoir of faith and good works. You are an anchor of devotion and loyalty and accomplishment. No one can gainsay the great part you play in the onward rolling of this work across the earth" (*Ensign*, November 1998, 97). In another setting he said, "I am confident that the daughters of God are as precious to Him as are His sons. They are as important a part of His eternal plan. It is obvious that there could be no continuity of the race without woman" (*New Era*, September 1988, 46).

From an eternal perspective, we know little about the reasons specific assignments were given to men and women, and little about the reason for the division of responsibilities between men and women in the gospel kingdom. Because of this the adversary seeks to create confusion about something that need not be confusing. He does this, in part, by attempting to divert our attention from what is really important. And what is important is eternal life and exaltation. The blessings of the priesthood—which include, but are not limited to, such blessings as the power to heal and bless, the power to hear the voice of the Spirit, the authority to baptize and endow, the authority to bind and seal generations, and certainly the power to exalt—are eternal and make anything this world has to offer pale by comparison. The blessings flowing from these powers, and many others, are available equally to righteous men and righteous women. In fact, the highest rewards the Father has for His children can be obtained only by a man and a woman *together*. The blessings of having an eternal family, of progressing eternally, and of eventually receiving exaltation together are all derived from the priesthood.

We also know that the Lord has declared His will on the matter of the division of responsibilities between men and women, and for reasons known to Him but not as yet revealed in their fulness to us, our assignments as sisters do not require that we be ordained to the priesthood, though the stewardship of worthy men does require ordination. This difference in the stewardship between the sons and daughters of God need not concern us. We should feel secure about the manner in which the Lord administers His kingdom.

I do. I do because I trust the Lord, and this is an issue of faith. This is *His* Church. He stands at its head. And it is inconsistent with the divine character of Jesus Christ to undermine or diminish the contribution or value of any of us. Our Father's plan assures that all our Father has is available to *all* who qualify, for "they who keep their second estate shall have glory added upon their heads for ever and ever" (Abraham 3:26), and those who seek the riches that it is the will of the Father to give them "shall be the richest of all people, for [they] shall have the riches of eternity" (D&C 38:39).

Regrettably, there are some men who hold the priesthood

who do not treat the women with whom they associate closely—including their wives, daughters, and those who serve as teachers and leaders in the Church—with the respect they deserve. But on this issue President Hinckley has been clear and definitive: "I regret that there are some men who are egotistical and evil, who are insensitive and even brutal. They are to be both condemned and pitied. I believe that any man who offends a daughter of God will someday be held accountable, and the time will come when he will stand before the bar of judgment with sorrow and remorse" (*Ensign,* November 1989, 95).

Gratefully, the offenses of a relative few do not negate the blessings or undermine the power of the priesthood, which is eternal, or the goodness of the majority of priesthood holders who stand as watchmen on the tower, who bear the priesthood worthily, and who exercise their responsibilities and priesthood privileges righteously.

I repeat: The blessings of the priesthood are available equally to righteous men and righteous women. President Joseph Fielding Smith explained that "the Lord offers to his daughters every spiritual gift and blessing that can be obtained by his sons" (*Improvement Era,* June 1970, 66). And Elder James E. Talmage's words add further understanding: "It is not given to woman to exercise the authority of the Priesthood independently; nevertheless, in the sacred endowments associated with the ordinances of the House of the Lord, woman shares with man the blessings of the Priesthood. . . . In the glorified state of the blessed hereafter, husband and wife will administer in their respective stations, seeing and understanding alike, and co-operating to the full in the government of their family kingdom. . . . Then shall woman reign by Divine right, a queen in the resplendent realm of her glorified state, even as exalted man shall stand, priest and king unto the Most High God. Mortal eye cannot see nor mind comprehend the beauty, glory, and majesty of a righteous woman made perfect in the celestial kingdom of God" (*Young Woman's Journal,* October 1914, 602).

All of us, men and women alike, receive the gift and gifts of the Holy Ghost and are entitled to personal revelation. We may *all* take upon us the Lord's name, become sons and daughters of Christ, partake of the ordinances of the temple from which we emerge armed with power (see D&C 109:22), receive the fulness of the gospel and a "fulness of the Holy Ghost" (D&C 109:15), and achieve exaltation in the celestial kingdom. These spiritual blessings emanate from the Melchizedek Priesthood, which holds the "keys of all the spiritual blessings of the church" (D&C 107:18).

As sisters we are not diminished by priesthood power, we are magnified by it. When respected and exercised righteously, this power unites rather than separates us. The Lord loves His sons *and* His daughters. Elder Talmage stated that "the world's greatest champion of woman and womanhood is Jesus Christ" (*Jesus the Christ,* 442). I believe it.

The first time we have record of the Lord acknowledging Himself to be the Christ, it was to a woman, a Samaritan woman no less, at Jacob's Well. After teaching her about Living Water, the Savior proclaimed, simply, "I . . . am he" (John 4:26).

It was Martha to whom the Lord declared: "I am the resurrection, and the life. . . . And whosoever liveth and believeth in me shall never die. Believest thou this?" Martha responded with the kind of faith countless believing women have exemplified throughout the history of the world: "Yea, Lord: I believe that thou art the Christ, the Son of God" (John 11:25–27).

Then, during His greatest agony as He hung on the cross, the Savior reached out to one person—His mother—when in that terrible but glorious moment He asked John the Beloved to care for her as though she were his own (see John 19:26–27).

And finally, it was a woman to whom He first showed Himself after rising from the tomb. "Touch me not;" He instructed Mary Magdalene, "for I am not yet ascended to my Father." He followed that request with a simple assignment, to go and find His Apostles and relay the news that He had risen! "Go to my brethren," He instructed, "and say unto them, I ascend unto my Father, and your Father; and to my God, and your God." Accordingly, "Mary Magdalene came and told the disciples that she had seen the Lord, and that he had spoken these things unto her" (John 20:17–18). Imagine! It was a woman who had the privilege of first seeing the Risen Lord, and then of relaying that news to the Twelve. Surely such an action bespeaks the Lord's reverence and respect for women.

Of this I am certain: The Lord *loves* and delights in righteous women—women who are not only faithful but filled with faith. Women who are optimistic and cheerful because they know who they are, who they have always been, and where they are going. Women who are striving to live and serve as women of God.

The penetrating question, then, related to the blessings of the priesthood is why more of us, men and women alike, don't more earnestly seek the blessings available by virtue of this transcendent power. Brigham Young declared that "we should learn how to take into our possession every blessing and every privilege that God has put within our reach" *(Discourses of Brigham Young,* 53). How, then, do we as women "take into our possession," or gain access to, the blessings of the priesthood?

Throughout modern revelation, particularly the Doctrine and Covenants, the word *receive* is used to mean "having faith in" or "accepting as true." Do not all of us, including we who are not ordained, *receive* or activate the blessings of the priesthood in our lives by our own faith and obedience—by *believing* the priesthood to be the power of God and having faith in its governance, by *seeking* those blessings and keeping sacred covenants, and by *sustaining* those who are ordained and called to lead us?

"For what doth it profit a man if a gift is bestowed . . . and he *receive* not the gift? Behold, he rejoices not in that which is given unto him, neither rejoices in him who is the giver of the gift" (D&C 88:33; emphasis added). Again from Brigham Young: "The Priesthood is given to the people . . . and, when properly understood, they may actually unlock the treasury of the Lord, and *receive* to their fullest satisfaction" *(Discourses of Brigham Young,* 131; emphasis added). Surely the "treasury of the Lord" includes the "wonders of eternity" (D&C 76:8) and the "riches of eternity" (D&C 38:39) that the Lord wishes to give us. Surely it includes the "mysteries of God" that are granted unto those who give Him heed and diligence (Alma 12:9). It is the power of the priesthood that makes it possible for us to *receive* the Holy Ghost and then learn to hear promptings conveyed by the Holy Ghost. It is the power of the priesthood that unlocks the door to heaven and allows us to understand the mysteries of God—or in other words, to understood how God works. The question we might therefore ask ourselves is, Are we *receiving* the privileges and unspeakable blessings associated with the gift of priesthood power by *believing, seeking,* and *sustaining?* And are we rejoicing in Him who gave the gift?

While on a Relief Society assignment in Cali, Colombia, with Carol Thomas of the Young Women general presidency, I had an unforgettable experience. We were finishing up a long evening of meetings, and because we were to catch a pre-dawn flight, the presiding stake president asked the congregation to remain seated while we departed. But upon the final "amen," several dozen priesthood leaders jumped to their feet and formed two lines, creating a pathway from the chapel outside to a waiting van. As we walked through this sheltered passageway, I found myself choking back tears. In that setting, there was no need to protect us physically. But the metaphor was clear. In that instance, priesthood leaders were symbolic of priesthood power. And it is the power of the priesthood that *marks* the path leading to eternal life, that *clears* the path, and that *protects* the path.

Within the priesthood is great power: the power to separate and safeguard us from the world, the power to subdue the adversary and surmount obstacles, the power to comfort, bless, and heal, the power to enlarge our physical and spiritual capacity and enable us to hear the voice of the Lord, the power to strengthen marriages and families and bind us to each other, and the power to triumph over mortality and come unto Him. These blessings may be received by *every* righteous, seeking son and daughter. As President Harold B. Lee taught, "Through the priesthood and only the priesthood may we . . . find our way back home" ("Be Loyal to the Royal within You," BYU Address, October 1957).

I can't imagine life without access to the blessings of the priesthood. Even as a girl I knew there was something magnificent and profound about this power, because when my father gave me blessings or performed ordinances, I could feel something I felt at no other time. Now, after years of seeking understanding in the scriptures and in the temple, I have come to know for myself, to know beyond doubt, that the priesthood is the power of God to bless and exalt every one of us—if we live worthy and seek its blessings. And that is what is important.

I had an experience in Recife, Brazil, while on Church assignment that demonstrated in a poignant way the influence of a priesthood leader magnifying his calling. For meetings there, I had a translator who was very skilled but also a bit nervous about doing side-by-side translation before a large audience of priesthood and auxiliary leaders. She had prepared herself by studying, fasting, and praying. The member of the Area Presidency under whose direction I was serving, Elder Claudio R. M. Costa, knew of her concerns. The meeting went well, and the translator did a beautiful job. It wasn't until afterward, however, that I learned "the rest of the story." A stake president seated on the stand told me what he had observed during the meeting: "I wish you could have seen Elder Costa and the Area Authority Seventy with him. They were on the edge of their seats, listening to everything you said and prompting the translator at times to make sure everything she said was a precise and faithful translation. When I said to Elder Costa, 'You were really *listening* to Sister Dew,' he said, 'Of course. She has brought a message from the Brethren, and it was my responsibility to make sure everyone heard it exactly as she meant it.'"

The Area Authority Seventy then told me, "You should know that Elder Costa told me that my assignment throughout the entire meeting was to pray for you and the translator. And so I did." My eyes instantly filled with tears. Though I was serving under Elder Costa's direction, as part of his leadership he in turn did everything he could to support and help me. Again, through the action of a worthy holder of the priesthood, I came to experience the support and protection of the *power* of the priesthood.

The power of the priesthood will be a vital source of strength and protection in our families and throughout the Church in the days ahead. The priesthood of God distinguishes the Lord's church from any other. Wherever and whenever its power and blessings are exercised, we may expect to find peace, security, directions, and protection—if we believe it to truly be the power of God and thus place ourselves in a position to receive the spiritual gifts and blessings that emanate from its power.

CHAPTER 10

FOLLOW THE PROPHET; HE KNOWS THE WAY

THE LIVING PROPHET WILL HELP US FIND THE WAY.
BUT IF WE DON'T LISTEN TO THE PROPHET,
WE MIGHT AS WELL NOT HAVE ONE.

ON THE FARM WE LEARNED TO DRIVE as soon as we could reach the pedals and see over the steering wheel, which for me was age ten; so by the time I was thirteen, I was a veteran behind the wheel. It was therefore not unusual when one winter Saturday during my eighth-grade year, Dad called up to the house from his shop and asked if I would drive his new pickup around to the back of the farm, adding a caution: "Sheri, be sure to scrape the windshield. It has a thick layer of ice on it."

Unfortunately, Dad had not summoned me at a convenient time. It was a Saturday afternoon in January, and I was doing what I did *every* Saturday afternoon in January—watching the Kansas University Jayhawks play basketball. To make matters worse, it was the fourth quarter and the game was on the line. But I had learned from sad experience that when Dad needed help, he meant now; so in sub-zero weather, I dashed out of the house in my shirtsleeves, ran to the pickup, and began chipping away at a stubborn layer of ice. Ten minutes later, when I had been able to clear only a small area about six inches in diameter, I was both frozen and frustrated because the game was going on without me.

Then, in a flash of thirteen-year-old wisdom, I decided it couldn't possibly hurt to drive the pickup the five hundred yards or so to Dad's shop. This was just the farm, for heaven's sakes. There probably wasn't another vehicle within miles. What could possibly go wrong?

So I hopped in the pickup and began to inch my way around to the back of the farm. But I was basically driving blind because that tiny hole allowed for no peripheral vision, and it quickly fogged over anyway. I hadn't gone fifty yards when I felt a thud and heard a sickening scraping sound. I slammed on the brakes, jumped out of the pickup, and immediately saw that I had hit our huge, ugly mailbox. The left mirror and trim dangled like limp appendages from the pickup body, and an ugly gash ran the length of the pickup bed. Instantly the basketball game faded in importance. I was horrified! Panicked! "Beam me up, Scotty!" I remember saying out loud in a spirit of desperation.

What happened from there is probably not important, other than to say that on several levels it turned out to be a painful experience—made all the more so because it need never have happened. Dad had warned me to scrape the windshield. But I had been impatient and focused on my own interests.

Just *one* of the lessons I learned from that incident (not meaning to slight those about obedience and patience and self-lessness) is that it is almost impossible to find your way if you can't even see the way, or to stay on the path if you can't see the path.

Further, when you can't see where you're going, there is no way to avoid the obstacles in front of you.

We are currently on a path designed to lead us home to our Heavenly Father, but that path is *littered* with obstacles that can be dangerous if not lethal. We are in trouble when our spiritual windshield is frosted over with anything: a preoccupation with the things of this world, pride, busyness, or out-and-out sin. In other words, there are many huge, ugly mailboxes along our path, each of them an invitation to temporal or spiritual disaster.

How often are we driving blind along the path of life, having scraped only a small clearing on our spiritual windshield, relying on our own wisdom rather than seeking counsel from those called to guide us and keep us in the center of the straight-and-narrow path?

Samuel the Lamanite delivered a stinging rebuke to the Nephites for rejecting the prophets in favor of self-appointed leaders who spoke flattering words and condoned their iniquities. "O ye wicked and ye perverse generation . . . how long will ye suffer yourselves to be led by foolish and *blind* guides? Yea, how long will ye choose darkness rather than light?" he declared (Helaman 13:29; emphasis added).

Mercifully, the Lord has not required us to find our way along the path alone. In addition to gifting us with the constant companionship of the Holy Ghost, with the magnificent power of the priesthood that blesses and protects us, and with the word of God as revealed by ancient prophets, He has provided us with a living prophet who testifies of and leads us to Christ, who Himself does not, indeed cannot "walk in crooked paths" (Alma 7:20).

There is nothing the world needs more than the message of

Jesus Christ. And there is no one in mortality who has the mantle to deliver that message more powerfully and with greater clarity than a prophet, for everything about a prophet points to and testifies of Christ. Prophets stand as the mortal link between man and God. Jesus Christ and His prophets are inseparably connected.

I have a friend who walks each morning with a nonmember neighbor who often raises moral and social issues on her mind. My friend, her walking partner, refers to this woman as her "deep-thinking friend." One morning as these two neighbors walked, the "deep-thinking friend" raised an issue that was bothering her. After a few minutes of discussion, she suddenly said to my friend (who at the time was serving as a stake Relief Society president), "I've been thinking about something you'll probably think is crazy, but I've been reading the Bible, and do you know what we really need? We need a prophet, like in ancient times, who can tell us how to handle these problems we can't seem to solve."

My friend's response was immediate: "I don't think you're crazy. In fact, I agree that only a prophet can help us find solutions to some of our difficult problems. But I must tell you that we have a prophet. And we receive guidance from him on a regular basis on issues such as the one you have raised." My friend's walking partner was amazed, curious, and eager to hear more, because the concept of a living prophet rang so true to her.

This leads to the question that we who believe—or profess to believe—in a living prophet might wish to ask ourselves. The question is, simply: *So what?* What difference does it make in our lives that a prophet walks the earth? When the prophet speaks, do we *do* anything differently? Do we modify behaviors or life patterns? Do we stop doing some things and begin doing others? In the fall of the year 2000, President Gordon B. Hinckley spoke in separate settings to the mothers, fathers, and youth of the Church. How many of us *heard* what he said—such that we have made changes in our lives?

Just prior to President Hinckley's fireside for youth, one of my nieces had pierced her ears a second time. After the fireside, she went home and took out the second pair of earrings. She admitted that she didn't really understand why wearing an extra set of earrings was a problem, but that if the prophet asked her to do it, that was good enough for her. Removing those earrings may or may not have eternal impact for this young woman, but her willingness to obey the prophet will. And if she'll obey him on a relatively simple issue, how much easier it will be to follow him when greater issues are at stake.

In short, living prophets point us to Christ and teach us truths about Him, including the following:

1. *This is the Lord's church, and He selects and prepares His prophets.*

Christ's church, which is "built upon the foundation of the apostles and prophets, Jesus Christ himself being the chief corner stone" (Ephesians 2:20), cannot exist without prophets and apostles. In all of scripture there is no evidence of the Lord identifying a people as His own and then failing to provide them with a prophet to communicate His will. And the implications of the merciful gift of a living prophet are stunning.

There aren't many guarantees in this life. There isn't a car made with a warranty that covers everything. No bank can guarantee that your money is safe. Even *Good Housekeeping's* seal of approval has a disclaimer of sorts on it. But that is to be expected, because nothing man-made can ever be guaranteed. Hence this miracle—and evidence of the Lord's mercy to His children—that *He* will choose the prophet, and that He will never let him lead us astray. It is an unimpeachable guarantee.

Prophets are not motivated by money or power. Their words haven't been polluted by the philosophies of men or by self-interest. Their objective is to take the gospel of Jesus Christ to every person who will listen, and then to help them live it. And their mission is to testify and bear witness of Christ. There is no source of information on earth as pure and unsullied. It is that simple. It is that profound.

The Lord is at the helm of his church, and nothing demonstrates that more than the manner in which He directs the selection and preparation of prophets. Said President Spencer W. Kimball, "[A new President is] not elected through committees and conventions, with all their conflicts, criticisms, and by the vote of men, but [is] called of God and then sustained by the people. . . . The pattern divine allows for no errors, no conflicts, no ambitions, no ulterior motives" *(Ensign,* January 1973, 33).

"Every man," said the Prophet Joseph, "who has a calling to minister to the inhabitants of the world was ordained to that very purpose in the Grand Council of heaven before this world was. I suppose that I was ordained to this very office in that Grand Council" *(Teachings,* 365).

Nowhere is the Lord's view of His children more apparent than in the selection of prophets, many of whom had humble beginnings. Elias was a farmer. Peter, James, and John were fishermen. Joseph Smith was an unschooled farm boy at the time of the First Vision. Brigham Young was a carpenter. Moses lamented the fact that he was "slow of speech, and of a slow tongue" (Exodus 4:10). Enoch was amazed when the Lord called him to serve as His mouthpiece. Truly, the Lord "seeth not as man seeth; for man looketh on the outward appearance, but the Lord looketh on the heart" (1 Samuel 16:7).

President George Q. Cannon said: "God has chosen [the prophet] to stand where he does—not you or me; and He knows every secret thought of men's hearts. His all-piercing eye has penetrated the innermost recesses of his heart, and He has seen all there is about him, inside and out. He knows him thoroughly, because He created him. He knew his past history; He knows his present history. And knowing this He has chosen him. What can we do better than to show respect to our God by listening to His servant, by treating him with reverence, asking his counsel and seeking for his guidance?" (*Gospel Truth*, 231).

The life of every prophet reveals not only his foreordination but his intense spiritual training, a tutorial designed and administered by the Divine Schoolmaster Himself. President J. Reuben Clark Jr. taught, "No man ever comes to lead God's people whom He has not trained for His task" (*Deseret News*, 5 May 1945).

A review of recent Church history bears this out. When President David O. McKay died at age ninety-six in January 1970, because of his lingering ill health and his age, it was a sad but expected day. Joseph Fielding Smith became president of the Church, and when he passed on eighteen months later at age ninety-three, again there was sadness but not great surprise. But when Harold B. Lee, who was then ordained president of the

Church at seventy-three, a relative youngster, died suddenly eighteen months later, the Church was stunned.

Elder William Grant Bangerter described the events that followed this way: "Suddenly [President Lee] was gone. . . . It was the first time since the death of the Prophet Joseph Smith when the president had died before it was time for him to die. . . . [Could] the Church survive this emergency? Of course, we knew that the Church would survive, but it could not possibly be the same. We had never expected Spencer W. Kimball to become the president, and we had not looked to him for the same leadership evident in the life of Harold B. Lee. We knew, of course, that he would manage somehow, until the next great leader arose, but . . . it would not be the same. 'O Lord,' we prayed, 'please bless President Kimball. He needs all the help you can give him.'"

Elder Bangerter then described what happened the first time President Kimball addressed the General Authorities. "As [President Kimball] proceeded with his address . . . he had not spoken very long when a new awareness seemed suddenly to fall on the congregation. We became alert to an astonishing spiritual presence, and we realized that we were listening to something unusual, powerful, different from any of our previous meetings. It was as if, spiritually speaking, our hair began to stand on end. . . . President Kimball spoke under this special influence for an hour and ten minutes. . . . When [he] concluded, President Ezra Taft Benson arose and . . . said, . . . 'President Kimball, through all the years that these meetings have been held, we have never heard such an address as you have just given. Truly, there is a prophet in Israel'" (*Ensign*, November 1977, 26–27).

Today, is there any question about the inspired leadership

that was provided by Spencer W. Kimball? The Lord knew then as He knows now who has been foreordained to lead the Church.

This same divinely inspired pattern is evident in the life of President Gordon B. Hinckley. At the time he was called to serve as a counselor to President Kimball in July 1981, both the first and second counselor in the First Presidency were in reasonably good health. Some might have wondered about the call of an additional counselor. But six weeks later President Kimball underwent his third brain surgery, from which he never completely recovered. And within a year and a half, President Marion G. Romney's health had deteriorated and President N. Eldon Tanner had died, at which time the weight and responsibility of conducting the affairs of the First Presidency fell almost entirely to President Hinckley. *What if* President Kimball had not extended the call to President Hinckley when he did? But there are no "what ifs" with the Lord, not when it comes to the leadership of His Church. As with each of his predecessors, everything about President Hinckley's life testifies of that fact.

Just one example of the Lord's hand in preparing President Hinckley is in the area of public relations. During his time as president of the Church, he has been interviewed by more journalists than all of his predecessors combined, including unprecedented network interviews with Mike Wallace and Larry King, and an appearance before the National Press Club. His deft ability to tell the Church's story under the camera's glare is remarkable. Consider the following interchanges with Mike Wallace during their interview for CBS's *60 Minutes.*

Mr. Wallace began their first interview by asking, "Mr. President, why did you agree to give us this rare interview?"

GBH: "Because I felt it was an opportunity to tell the people of America something about this great cause in which I have such a keen interest."

Wallace: "But that is not traditional with Mormons."

GBH: "Oh, I don't know."

Wallace: "Can you tell me the last president of the Mormon Church who went on nationwide television to do an interview with no questions ahead of time so that you know what is coming?"

GBH: "No, I don't remember one."

Wallace: "So, Gordon Hinckley decided, apparently, that there is a message that the Mormon Church has for America and, for that matter, the world."

GBH: "Yes, indeed."

Wallace: "And that message is?"

(Freeze frame for a moment. The camera is rolling and there's time for only a sound-bite. How does one respond to such an all-encompassing question? President Hinckley said this:)

GBH: "That message is that there is a way to greater peace. There is a way to greater harmony in our living. . . . There is a way to improve things. That is what I would like to say."

Here's another exchange:

Wallace: "You have retained a public relations agency. . . . Is that to proselytize, . . . or to tell the rest of us heathens what we are missing?"

GBH: "It is to tell the rest of you what you are missing, yes."

Wallace: "And what is it that we are missing?"

(Now, again, with just a few seconds to answer, how would you respond?)

GBH: "You are missing the lift that comes of living close to the Lord, walking with faith and with purpose, with a feeling that life is really purposeful, that it is a mission rather than just a career. There is something wonderful about having some concept of who you are, as a [child] of God, with a divine destiny, and the knowledge that you can make more of your life than you may have been making of it."

When asked if he believed in an afterlife, President Hinckley responded, "I certainly do. I think life after this life is as certain as life here. I believe we lived before we came here, that we live here for a purpose—"

"Wait, wait," Wallace interrupted. "You believe we lived before we came here?"

"Oh, absolutely, as intelligences, as spirits," President Hinckley replied.

"There was a spirit of Gordon Hinckley?" Wallace asked.

"Absolutely, and of Mike Wallace."

"I hope not," Wallace joked.

Now notice the way President Hinckley introduces the concept of an eternal plan: "Life is an eternal thing, Mike. It is part of an eternal plan, our Father's plan for His sons and daughters, whom He loves. His work and His glory is to bring about the immortality and eternal life of His sons and daughters. It has purpose. It is meaningful."

When asked how he accounted for the rapid growth of a church that was so demanding of its people, President Hinckley turned a perceived negative into a positive: "Yes, it is demanding. And that is one of the things that attracts people to this Church. It stands as an anchor in a world of shifting values. They feel they have something solid that they are standing on while the ground is moving beneath them. People are looking for something of substance and strength, based on eternal truth and eternal values."

Clearly the Lord magnified President Hinckley during this sensitive interview. But the Lord sustained him not only during the interview itself but through decades of preparation, beginning seventy years earlier when, as a young returned missionary, he was named to sit with six members of the Twelve on the first Church committee assigned to develop tracts and filmstrips for missionaries. Imagine the tutoring he received from Elders Stephen L Richards, John A. Widtsoe, and others as they designed ways to tell the Church's story to the world.

In addition, repeatedly during more than forty years as a General Authority, Elder Hinckley was assigned to handle nearly every sensitive issue that arose with the press: Utah's debate over liquor-by-the-drink, the MX missile controversy, the clash over the Equal Rights Amendment, priesthood restrictions to African-Americans, forged historical documents that called into question the veracity of Joseph Smith's story, and so on. When the Church celebrated its sesquicentennial in 1980, whom did President Kimball assign to appear on *The Today Show* with Tom Brokaw? Elder Hinckley. Very simply, for years the Lord had been tutoring him and providing opportunities to "practice" the craft of presenting the Church's message to the world. Thus, as president of the Church in an age dominated by around-the-clock media coverage, his skills and life experience are allowing him to fulfill his unique mission. As Elder Neal A. Maxwell told a group of missionaries: "You are the first generation to see the globalization of the Church. No one has played a greater role in that effort than President Hinckley" (Dew, *Go Forward with Faith*, 547).

What a magnificent source of security, in a society whose underpinnings are constantly shifting and whose leadership so often rests in the hands of the most articulate or charismatic rather than the most trustworthy, to know that the Lord prepares and then puts in place the man foreordained to lead us!

On occasion there have been those who advocated removing an aging president from office in favor of a more energetic leader. Such a suggestion results from either a lack of understanding or phenomenal arrogance. The gospel kingdom is not a democracy. The Lord has not invited us to nominate candidates but to indicate our support of His anointed. Were it not so, the Church would be no different from any other institution, religious or secular. The president of the Church doesn't become such throughout campaigning or because of his earthly qualifications, but because He has the endorsement of the Lord.

2. Prophets are living witnesses that faith, hope, and charity are fundamental characteristics of followers of Christ.

There is no faith unless it is in Jesus Christ. Otherwise, it is only a belief or an idea, neither of which has the power to save. What Christ requires first is that we *believe* in Him. The Apostle Paul said that "without faith it is impossible to please [God]: for he that cometh to God must believe that he is, and that he is a rewarder of them that diligently seek him" (Hebrews 11:6).

Without exception, prophets are men of profound faith. Captain Moroni's unflagging trust in the Lord allowed him to lead the Nephites to victory against the larger, stronger Lamanite armies. When the Prophet Joseph was seized upon by a dark, unseen power in the Sacred Grove, he instinctively called upon God for deliverance (see JS–H 1:16). It was faith that enabled Brigham Young to lead his weary band of Saints to an uncharted, uncultivated desert in the West.

President Hinckley has also repeatedly turned to the Lord in faith. A journal entry he made while serving as President Kimball's counselor reveals his dependence upon the Lord: "The responsibility I carry frightens me. . . . I pray each day for strength and wisdom and inspiration. . . . Sometimes I could weep with concern. But there comes the assurance that the Lord put me here for His purpose, and if I will be humble and seek the direction of the Holy Spirit, He will use me according to His will to accomplish His purposes" (Dew, *Go Forward with Faith*, 393). Repeatedly he has said, "Walk by faith. . . . When there is no way, [God] will open the way" (*Teachings of Gordon B. Hinckley*, 196).

On the same day in April 1961 that Elder Hinckley offered a prayer inaugurating missionary work in the Philippines, he received a rejection on the application he had filed in behalf of the Church for visas allowing missionaries to enter the country. Borrowing a typewriter, he went to his hotel room and wrote a lengthy reply to emigration officials, noting: "We must now pray and wait. However it is in the hands of the Lord. We shall do our best and await the outcome. If we cannot get what we need through one channel we shall try every other until we secure the proper entry documents. . . . Somehow it will go forward. This is the Lord's work and while it may be delayed, it will not be stopped" (Dew, *Go Forward with Faith*, 227).

A few months later, having rejoiced when the way opened to obtain the necessary visas, he returned with the first four missionaries assigned to Manila. Sister Hinckley accompanied him. As they prepared to leave, her mothering instincts momentarily got the best of her, and she asked, "You're not really going to leave those four boys here alone in this huge city, are you?" His reply was immediate: "They are not alone. The Lord is with them."

Faith in Christ carries with it the assurance that we are not alone. Faith is also the seedbed of hope, for true hope is always the result of faith in Christ. Though all prophets know sacrifice and loneliness, their bedrock faith in Christ allows them to hope for not only the best in this world but the glorious reality of eternal life.

President Hinckley's confidence in the Divine has given him a buoyant optimism that has governed his attitude about life and its myriad of challenges. When for example in the mid-1960s an anxious mission president wrote to report that monsoon rains had damaged both the mission home and his spirits, Elder Hinckley replied, "Needless to say this was a frightening experience. . . . You may be interested to know that the night before the London Temple was dedicated we had a flood of serious proportions there. I stood in water to my waist . . . bailing it out. This went on for hours. I only want to suggest that your experience is not peculiar. . . . Noah had a worse time. Sincerely, your brother" (Dew, *Go Forward with Faith*, 287).

When confronted by challenge, President Hinckley typically utters his trademark phrase, "Things will work out." This statement to General Authorities is indicative of countless others: "We have critics, not a few. They come and go. They do little hurt to anyone but themselves. It all works out to the blessing of the work. This has become the motto of my life. *It will all work out.* ... We are in the hands of the Almighty, whose cause this is. ... He who is our God, and whose Church this is, will prevail" (meeting with General Authorities, 3 April 1997).

As faith increases, and hope fills our souls, our concern for others intensifies. The natural extension of faith and hope is charity, the pure love of Christ. Said the Prophet Joseph, "The nearer we get to our heavenly Father, the more we are disposed to look with compassion on perishing souls" (*History of the Church,* 5:24). Just as Christ ministered one by one to those in need, His prophets have an overarching concern for every individual. That is just one of the reasons President Kimball petitioned the Lord with such fervor regarding the ordination of *all* worthy males to the priesthood. It is just one of the reasons President Hinckley has *pleaded* with us repeatedly to welcome each new member into the embrace of the Church and to help them make the transition that inevitably accompanies baptism.

3. *Prophets mirror the humility of the Master.*

Jesus Christ, the Savior of the world, performed the ultimate act of submission. Consider His role in the premortal council where, after Satan offered to redeem all mankind in return for the honor, Christ proclaimed to the Father, "Thy will be done, and the glory be thine forever" (Moses 4:2).

Consider the humility of Joseph Smith, who saw Deity and conversed with angels, but who recognized that he did not have the authority to organize a church or confer priesthood ordinances until he received such authority from on high. Said President George Q. Cannon, "There are few men ... who, if they had obtained the gifts that he possessed, would not have overstepped the limit of their calling and authority and done something beyond their province. But Joseph did not err in this way" (*Gospel Truth*, 198).

Prophets mirror the humility of Him whose servants they are. It is not that they are unaware of their skills and native talents. It is simply that they realize where their talents come from and to Whom they belong. Their focus has shifted from themselves and their own importance to the work of the Lord and its transcendent importance.

As President Hinckley said to a group of young adults, "Don't be arrogant. The world is full of arrogant people. . . . How obnoxious is an arrogant man!" (CES Young Adult Meeting, 14 April 1996). He, like other prophets, has managed to avoid the arrogance trap. Consider the sentiment he expressed to his Brethren of the General Authorities: "I just cannot get over the tremendous responsibility we have. There has been laid upon us as people of ordinary talent the work of carrying the gospel of Jesus Christ to all the world. . . . I just speak of myself and wonder if I should be doing a little more" (meeting with General Authorities, 9 October 1996).

Indeed, President Hinckley and other prophets follow the pattern of the Savior: "And whosoever will be chief among you, let him be your servant: Even as the Son of man came not to be ministered unto, but to minister, and to give his life a ransom for many" (Matthew 20:27–28).

4. *There is order in the Lord's kingdom, and the only safety in this world is in following the prophet, the Lord's anointed.*

One of the reassuring lessons from the First Vision is that the heavens are open and that God speaks to those who will listen.

Nonetheless, there must be order in the Lord's kingdom. Therefore, when the Lord has something to say to His people as a whole, He will say it through His prophet, for "there is never but one on the earth at a time on whom this power and the keys of this priesthood are conferred" (D&C 132:7). This fundamental principle of order eliminates confusion as well as the jockeying for position that occurs in every organization created and directed by man.

The Lord through His prophet will keep us informed. The question is, Are we listening? The story is told that Brigham Young, after having urged the people in certain communities to clean up their properties, refused to go back to preach to them, saying something along these lines: "You didn't listen to me last time when I urged you to fix up your premises. The same doors are off their hinges; the same barns are still unpainted; the same fences are partly fallen. I will return when you are ready for the next sermon but you haven't done anything about the first one yet" (See *1978 Devotional Speeches of the Year*, 136).

If we don't listen to the prophet, we might as well not have one. Said President Harold B. Lee, "The men who preside in this church are only prophets to those who accept them and their teachings as the prophecies from the living God" (BYU Devotional Address, 3 October 1950).

A while ago I found a copy of a talk I gave when I was about nine. The talk, "Yes. Wilco. Mobile Now. Out," was about following the prophet. This is what I wrote so long ago: "*Yes,* President McKay, I have received your message. *Wilco,* I will comply with your request. *Mobile now.* I am going to start and do it right now—not when I get time, but right now. *Out!* I don't need any further convincing—the fact that you suggested it is good enough, because I know you are a phrophet [sic] of God."

Nearly forty years later, I can't improve on that message. Again, *if we don't listen to the prophet, we might as well not have one.* Do we know what President Hinckley has said about strengthening our families, about getting out of debt, about abortion and spouse abuse and pornography, about pierced ears and the roles of fathers and mothers? Have we as sisters studied the magnificent addresses he gave at the 1998 and 2000 General Relief Society Meetings, which set a standard for every Latter-day Saint woman? Again, from Elder Harold B. Lee: "Every soul today that is not hearkening unto the . . . inspired counsel that comes from the [Lord's] leaders is being deceived by the power of Satan, and they are gradually coming to be in his power. . . . Satan never goes on vacation. He never sleeps" (*Children's Friend,* June 1949, 254–55).

History has repeatedly demonstrated the wisdom of following the prophet. Consider the events of 1837. The previous year the Kirtland Temple had been dedicated, and a magnificent outpouring of the Spirit had increased the faith of the Saints. But soon the adversary began moving with renewed determination through the Church, and many apostatized. Dissension threatened to sap the lifeblood of the Church. It was in this climate that Joseph Smith went to Heber C. Kimball in the Kirtland Temple and said, "Brother Heber, the Spirit of the Lord has whispered to me: Let my servant Heber go to England and proclaim my Gospel" (*History of the Church,* 2:490). Joseph's declaration made no sense. Heber was one of his most loyal advocates. Surely Joseph needed him at his side. It was like a CEO sending his board of directors away with their company on the verge of a hostile takeover.

But Heber accepted the Prophet's call, as did others of the Twelve. With faith and little else (Heber had five dollars in his pocket), they left for England. In time, the Lord's reasoning and the Prophet's wisdom would become obvious. For the mission of the Twelve to England in the late 1830s proved critical to the growth and stability of the Church. It was the infusion of thousands of British Saints into the weakened body of the Church in the early 1840s that revived it. Who, with the Church in such precarious condition, would have sent his most trusted advisors an ocean away? Only a prophet who knew what the Church and its people needed in that day.

Fast-forward to 1844 and 1845. The Prophet Joseph was gone, and mobs were terrorizing Nauvoo. The Saints were emotionally, physically, and spiritually spent. The temple, which they had been commanded to build, wasn't completed. Who would have dared say to that bedraggled group, "Load up, we're going west to a place the Lord has shown me." The Lord's presiding high priest, who knew what the Church and its people needed in that day.

Again, fast-forward to the 1980s when an emotional debate raged over the proposed Equal Rights Amendment. On the surface, it seemed to some that this bill would only benefit women, particularly those who worked outside the home—until a prophet spoke and exposed the subtle distortions embedded in that legislation that threatened to undermine and blur the divine distinctions between men and women. Who could have seen through the political and social fog and understood so clearly the negative ramifications of that bill? A prophet of God relaying information from the Lord.

It was President Ezra Taft Benson who said that "God's revelations to Adam did not instruct Noah how to build the Ark. Noah needed his own revelation" (*BYU Speeches of the Year*, 1980, 26).

Those who are willing to heed and hear a prophet's voice will find it almost impossible to stray from the path or to hit the mailboxes along the way. A favorite Primary song expresses it well: "Now we have a world where people are confused. If you don't believe it, go and watch the news. We can get direction all along our way, if we heed the prophets—follow what they say. Follow the prophet, follow the prophet, follow the prophet . . . he knows the way" (*Children's Songbook*, 111).

President Harold B. Lee said much the same thing: "We have some tight places to go before the Lord is through with this church and the world in this dispensation. . . . The power of Satan will increase; we see it in evidence on every hand. . . . The only safety we have as members of this Church is to . . . give heed to the . . . commandments that the Lord shall give through His prophet. . . . You may not like what comes from the authority of the Church. It may contradict your political views. It may contradict your social views. . . . But if you listen to these things, as if from the mouth of the Lord Himself, . . . the promise is that 'the gates of hell shall not prevail against you'" (in Conference Report, October 1970, 152–53). It may be that *the most vital* lesson we can learn ourselves and then teach our children and families in this critical era is to follow the prophet.

5. Jesus is the Christ, and His atonement is the supreme act and gift in time and eternity.

Every prophet from Adam to the current day has testified that Christ will lift us up, if we will let Him (see Moroni 9:25–26). He will lift our sights, sharpen our vision, bless us with hope and peace of mind, and strengthen us with the resolve to rise above the world. It was so as the Nephite civilization crumbled. It is so today, as the moral underpinnings of our society rot with decay. The only answer to the challenge of mortality—the only place we can find the strength and peace we must have—is in the Lord Jesus Christ, whose atonement not only paid the price for sin but compensated for all of the pain and bitterness we face along this part of the path.

The preeminent witness of Christ in this dispensation is the Prophet Joseph, whose testimony of the Father and the Son is the wellspring of The Church of Jesus Christ of Latter-day Saints: "And now, after the many testimonies which have been given of him, this is the testimony, last of all, which we give of him: That he lives! For we saw him, even on the right hand of God" (D&C 76:22–23).

Joseph's successors have likewise stood as witnesses of Christ, and the fruits of their labors speak for themselves. The Church continues to march steadily forward, as President Hinckley has often said, with never a backward step. Its history is heroic. Its members are a covenant people. Temples are dotting the earth. This work hasn't been led by idle dreamers. It has been led by prophets of God.

President Hinckley has urged us forward with these words: "The time has come for us to stand a little taller, to lift our eyes and stretch our minds to a greater . . . understanding of the grand millennial mission of this The Church of Jesus Christ of Latter-day Saints. This is a season to be strong. It is a time to move forward without hesitation" (*Ensign*, May 1995, 71).

The days ahead promise high adventure as well as spiritual challenges that will rival anything the world has ever seen. At times the path we are on will feel tight and narrow. And the path will ever be littered with big, ugly mailboxes. But if we will keep our spiritual windshield clear so that we can keep our eye on the prophet, we will stay on course.

What difference does it make that we have a prophet? It makes all the difference. Either we have a prophet, or we don't. If we don't, we have nothing. If we do, we have everything. Joseph saw what he said he saw in a grove of trees in upstate New York. It is because of him that we know why we're here, where we're going, and that we have on earth a prophet who will lead us there.

It has been my privilege to spend time with two presidents of the Church—President Ezra Taft Benson and President Gordon B. Hinckley—in the preparation of their biographies. Never have I been with either of these men that the Spirit has not made me aware, instantly, that I was in the presence of a prophet of God.

The message of this millennium is that Jesus is the Christ, that His gospel has been restored in its fulness to the earth, and that we are led by a prophet who will help us find our way.

CHAPTER 11

THE PARABLE
OF PANMUNJOM

NOTHING BRINGS MORE PEACE OF MIND, SECURITY,

AND SAFETY THAN LIVING

ON THE LORD'S SIDE OF THE LINE.

W HEN I WAS A STUDENT AT BYU, I took a year off
from my studies to tour with a professional USO
group that entertained at military bases around the
world. One trip took us to the Far East, and before we left, my
father gave me a strong warning. "I am worried about this trip,"
he said. "If something were to happen to you, we might never get
you back. Be careful. Don't go anywhere you shouldn't go." This
wasn't the first time I had been out of the country, and his words
caught me by surprise. But, frankly, as our adventure in the exotic
Orient began, I forgot about his warning—until, that is, one day
when we were scheduled to perform at a military base near the
Demilitarized Zone that separated North and South Korea.

When our escort officer asked if we would like to go into the
DMZ and visit Panmunjom, where the peace treaty ending the
Korean War had been signed, I was instantly interested. I was a
history major, and this was a place of great historical significance.
Relations between the two Koreas were strained at the time,

however, and we asked if it was safe. The officer assured us it was, but then promptly furnished waivers we were to sign absolving the military of responsibility in the event of accident or death. I suddenly remembered Dad's warning: "*Be careful. Don't go anywhere you shouldn't go.*" But not wanting to be the killjoy, and being curious myself, I shrugged off my worry, signed the waiver, and headed into the DMZ, where we were no longer under the protection of the U.S. Armed Forces.

That reality was immediately evident as we drove past rows of somber North Korean soldiers sporting machine guns. "Don't look them in the eyes," we were warned. "Anything can set them off." As we joked about our bodies never being found, my stomach started to churn and my father's warning played in my mind in digital, Dolby sound. I knew that I had indeed gone somewhere I shouldn't have gone. The experience was nerve-racking. I felt as though I was behind enemy lines. As fascinating as the excursion was, I couldn't wait to get out of there. It wasn't until we crossed the border back into South Korea that I again felt a measure of peace. And, as it turns out, for good reason. Later that week three Americans were shot in the Demilitarized Zone.

With this experience in mind, consider these words from George Albert Smith, delivered when he was a member of the Quorum of the Twelve: "There is a division line well defined that separates the Lord's territory from Lucifer's. If we live on the Lord's side of the line Lucifer cannot come there to influence us, but if we cross the line into his territory we are in his power. By keeping the commandments of the Lord we are safe on His side of the line, but if we disobey His teachings we <u>voluntarily</u> cross into the zone of temptation and invite the destruction that is ever present there. Knowing this, how anxious we should always be to live on the Lord's side of the line" (*Improvement Era*, May 1935, 278).

If we live on the Lord's side of the line, Lucifer cannot come there to influence us. What an offer of safety and security in a world that Lucifer has turned into enemy-occupied territory; a world where his enticements are more provocative and enslaving than ever; a world where he will resort to *any* tactic to lure us to his side of the line where we are no longer under the influence and protection of the Holy Ghost. Fortunately, Satan can't *make* us do anything. The Prophet Joseph said: "As well might the devil seek to dethrone Jehovah, as overthrow an innocent soul that resists everything which is evil" (*History of the Church*, 4:605).

And everyone has the power to resist evil. "It is true that some have greater power of resistance than others," said Elder George Q. Cannon, "but everyone has the power to close his heart against doubt, against darkness, against unbelief, against depression, against anger, against hatred, against jealousy, against malice, against envy. God has given this power unto all of us, and we can gain still greater power by calling upon Him for that which we lack" (*Gospel Truth*, 1:16).

Thus, the only power the adversary has is power we *give* him when we intentionally or knowingly sin or break our covenants. Happily, we have not been left to withstand the wiles of the adversary unaided, for the power of Jesus Christ is stronger than the power of the devil. Hence we have the promise that Lucifer cannot influence us when we stay on the Lord's side of the line. No wonder we are counseled, "Pray always lest that wicked one have power in you, and *remove you out of your place*" (D&C 93:49;

emphasis added). No wonder we have been admonished, "Stand ye in holy places, and *be not moved*" (D&C 87:8; emphasis added).

Very simply, our physical and spiritual safety lies in never even getting close to the line that separates light from dark, good from evil. Jesus Christ showed us how to deal with the adversary. When Satan tempted Him, there was no clever repartee or debate, no battle of wills, just immediate dismissal: "Get thee behind me, Satan. . . . Thou shalt not tempt the Lord thy God" (Luke 4:8, 12). If the omniscient Jehovah wasn't willing to debate the adversary, how quickly ought we to run for our lives—our eternal lives—when confronted with even the slightest hint of evil.

By and large, the men and women of this Church are bright and capable. But none of us is *that* smart. None of us is resilient enough to tango with the adversary. We can *never* match his cunning or his talent for deception and diversion. He will outsmart, outmaneuver, and outlast us every time we willingly consent to a duel. Lucifer is like the ultimate carnival barker: "Step right up. Come on in. Don't miss the greatest show on earth." But as soon as he has you inside his tent, he will leave you to twist in agony and isolation and darkness.

Happily, the choice about which side of the line we stand on is ours, for we "are free to choose liberty and eternal life, through the great Mediator . . . , or to choose captivity and death, according to the captivity and power of the devil" (2 Nephi 2:27). The choice is ours. If we will allow Him to, Jesus Christ will shield and deliver us from Lucifer, who because of his rebellion and arrogance and thirst for power forfeited his inheritance and is now bent on jeopardizing ours. How crucial it therefore is that we become steadfast and immovable on the Lord's side of the line, where we are not only protected but ultimately sealed up unto the Lord (see Mosiah 5:15).

The principle of being steadfast and immovable reminds me of the North Carolina Tar Heels. As a product of the great basketball state of Kansas, I have watched many a ball game between the K. U. Jayhawks and the Tar Heels, and that unusual mascot—the Tar Heels—has always intrigued me. When I found out the genius of the phrase *Tar Heels,* I was even more impressed. During the Civil War those tough Carolina farm boys refused to concede ground to the Union army, and it came to be said that they stood as though they had tar on their heels. They would not budge.

Being steadfast and immovable with our heels in tar on the Lord's side of the line is the only strategy that will work long term against Lucifer. Some of his enticements are blatant and cause those who succumb to take giant leaps into his territory. *Any breach of morality is immorality. Anything that isn't honest is dishonest.* Any exposure to pornography, drugs, alcohol, and even excessive materialism is championed by the father of lies.

Breaches of integrity, large and small, are always associated with leaps onto Lucifer's side of the line. Just prior to the 2000 presidential election, I was assigned to speak to a professional, East-coast organization about the subject of leadership. Because a large portion of the audience were members of the Church, I approached the topic by discussing what we could learn about leadership from prophets of God, whom I consider the ultimate in mortal (and moral) leadership. Drawing from the lives of prophets ancient and modern, we discussed fundamental characteristics of true leadership, and naturally one of the characteristics was integrity. After the seminar, a prominent professional woman, a nonmember, approached me and said, "You know, I've never given much thought to the notion that we ought to expect our leaders to be honest, but I can see now that organizations fall apart when people don't tell the truth."

I found it startling that someone so accomplished professionally would never have considered the question of ethics and honesty in any setting, let alone our government. But then, recent events on the national political and social stage would suggest there are many whose attitudes reflect that woman's. Ten years ago the word *spin* meant what happens inside one of Disneyland's famous teacups. Today the word means coloring and shading the facts to prove whatever position you want to prove.

There is nothing new about dishonesty. There is nothing creative or clever or admirable about the breach of one's integrity. After Cain had slain Abel, the Lord asked him where his brother was. In response, Cain both lied and tried to divert attention away from himself: "I know not," he said. "Am I my brother's keeper?" (Genesis 4:9). Dishonesty didn't work then, and it doesn't work now. The Lord knew better. "What hast thou done? the voice of thy brother's blood crieth unto me from the ground. And now art thou cursed from the earth" (Genesis 4:10–11). Cain's troubles began with pride and jealousy, but they were fueled by dishonesty.

How serious is dishonesty? Satan himself is often called the father of lies because his tactics always involve prevarication, deception, and, yes, "spin." Said President Gordon B. Hinckley: "In our day . . . those found in dishonesty [are not] put to death for their misdeeds, as in biblical times. But something within them dies. Conscience chokes, character withers, self-respect vanishes, integrity dies" (*Standing for Something*, 16).

Society begins to collapse when people don't tell the truth. Dishonesty corrodes companies, creates toxic corporate cultures, destroys unity and love within a family, wrecks relationships, mauls marriages, undermines unity in any setting, and leads always to breaking other commandments. Always. That is why the adversary is bent on attacking our integrity in ways large and small.

If he can't get us to succumb to blatant evil, he tries to coax us onto his side of the line by resorting to strategies that are sometimes more difficult to detect—strategies that slowly wear us down, weaken our resolve, and dim our memory of who we are. Whenever we succumb to the adversary's tactics, be they blatant or subtle, we experience what I did that day in the DMZ—fear and anxiety—because with all of his cunning, the adversary cannot duplicate joy or peace. That is why there is such safety on the Lord's side of the line, where the power of the priesthood and the Holy Ghost protect us.

So how do we stay on the Lord's side of the line? How do we stand in holy places and be not moved? In the twenty-first century there is a great deal we can learn from Helaman and his two thousand stripling warriors. The story is a familiar one. Two thousand righteous young men stepped forward to fight in the stead of their fathers, who had made a covenant never again to shed the blood of their brethren (see Alma 24:18). These young men were ultimately victorious against a larger, more experienced Lamanite army for several reasons:

1. *Before the sons of Helaman began their campaign, they entered into a covenant.* These young men covenanted "that they never would give up their liberty, but they would fight in all cases to

protect the Nephites and themselves from bondage" (Alma 53:17). It is the same with us. The first step toward consecration and total commitment to the Lord is making covenants with Him. That is what we do at baptism. That is what we do again later, with powerful spiritual ramifications, when we enter the house of the Lord.

There is *power* in making covenants. Weekly, as we renew our covenants and promise to take upon ourselves the name of the Son, to always remember Him, and to keep His commandments, we receive in return a transcendent promise, one filled with heavenly power: that we "may always have his Spirit to be with [us]" (Moroni 4:3). Having the Holy Ghost with us—and learning to hear His voice—is a key, perhaps the single most profound key, to remaining steadfast and immovable on the Lord's side of the line. And it all begins by making a covenant.

2. *The two thousand stripling warriors not only made covenants, they kept them.* Not only is there power in making covenants, there is even greater power in keeping them. Helaman's youthful band "were men who were true at all times in whatsoever thing they were entrusted" (Alma 53:20). In short, they did what they said they would do. They weren't always looking for ways to straddle the line between right and wrong, or to fudge on their commitments.

After President Hinckley was interviewed by Mike Wallace for *60 Minutes,* I had occasion to talk with Mr. Wallace about their conversation. Of all the things he mentioned admiringly about President Hinckley, it seemed that Mr. Wallace was most impressed with the fact that President Hinckley had done everything in connection with the interview that he had promised to do. When I later offered to show Mr. Wallace how I intended to quote him in President Hinckley's biography, he replied, "That's not necessary. You're a Mormon. I trust you." Do you really think this seasoned journalist believes that *every* member of the Church is trustworthy? Of course not. He is not that naive. His expression was not a reflection of me or even of the Church at large; it was a reflection of his experience with President Hinckley. In effect, he was saying, "If you are associated with *that* man, then I assume that you, too, will do what you have said you will do."

The integrity of another modern-day prophet, President Ezra Taft Benson, also caught the attention of the press. When Elder Ezra Taft Benson was serving as Secretary of Agriculture under President Dwight D. Eisenhower, his agricultural policies often took a beating on Capitol Hill and therefore in the media. But at the same time his policies were criticized, his moral fiber and character were repeatedly championed, as they were in one *New York Times Magazine* article: "One reason [for Secretary Benson's inner calm] is his religion. . . . He acts like a man whose conscience is always clear—his testimony [before Congress] today will be the same next week or the week after or a year from now. He doesn't have to remember what he said to an opposition Senator at their last meeting. This is a built-in ulcer-saving device not always found in Washington" (Dew, *Ezra Taft Benson*, 295–96). A reporter from *American* magazine asked him his secret, and Elder Benson replied, "It's easy to keep calm if you have inner security and peace of mind. . . . I try to do the thing I believe to be right and let the chips fall where they will." In fact, Elder Benson often told his Capitol Hill colleagues, "I feel it is always good strategy to stand up for the right, even when it is unpopular. Perhaps I should say, especially when it is unpopular" (Dew, *Ezra Taft Benson*, 296, 303.)

Are we true at all times to the things with which we have been entrusted? Do we stand up for the right, even when it is unpopular? Do we do something so simple and basic as tell the truth? Are we true to those who have trusted us with their love and their confidence? Are we true to the knowledge that we are sons and daughters of God with an eternal future? Are we true to the whisperings of the Spirit? Are we true to our temple covenants? Are we doing what we promised we would do before we came here and promised again when we were baptized and endowed?

The stripling warriors not only kept their covenants but performed "every word of command with exactness" (Alma 57:21). In other words, they kept their covenants with precision. A half-hearted effort to keep the Sabbath day holy or to be morally clean or to tell the truth or to dress modestly is really no effort at all. Joseph Smith didn't say that we *sort of* believe in being "honest, true, chaste, benevolent, [and] virtuous" (Articles of Faith 1:13). On Mount Sinai the Lord didn't declare, "Thou shalt not steal—unless you're in a real bind." He didn't say, "Thou shalt *rarely* covet." He didn't say, "Thou shalt not commit adultery—very often." He said, *"Thou shalt not,"* clearly delineating lines we are not to cross—lines that represent breaches in integrity or morality or virtue so serious that they drive the Spirit away and lead ultimately to the destruction of our souls; lines to stay away from lest we lose control of our thoughts, our motives, or our actions and step into Lucifer's territory where we come under his control.

Men and women who sell their birthright for a mess of

pottage almost universally confess that their demise began with something small, with some seemingly insignificant breach of integrity that escalated. The little things *do* matter. It is not possible to profess righteousness while flirting with sin. Believe me, Lucifer wants those of the noble birthright. He wants our minds and our bodies and our souls. I daresay there is no greater smirking in the underworld than when he gets his chains around a man or woman who has made sacred covenants.

It is as we keep the commandments and our covenants with exactness that the Lord strengthens us. The supreme example is the Savior Himself. In Gethsemane, after He renewed His covenant to follow through on the most dramatic but vital commitment associated with this earth—a commitment critical and central to our Father's plan—saying, "Not my will, but thine, be done," *after* that, "there appeared an angel unto him from heaven, strengthening him" (Luke 22:42–43) so that He could endure what lay ahead. On the cross when He uttered the words, "It is finished, thy will is done" (JST, Matthew 27:54; see also John 19:30), He became the greatest example in time or eternity of keeping covenants. There would have been no Atonement had the Lord not kept His covenant precisely as He promised. It is the same with us. As we recommit ourselves, the Lord strengthens us to withstand any temptation.

Living as Latter-day Saints is not easy. But it is easier than the alternative. The cost of discipleship, as high as it may be, is less than the price of sin—less costly than having the Holy Ghost withdraw or losing self-respect or jeopardizing eternal life.

3. *The stripling warriors were believers.* Their faith in Christ was active and dynamic. They believed that He could move

mountains—not to mention battalions of bloodthirsty Lamanites bent on their destruction—if they had faith in Him. Thus, when asked to put their lives on the line, they responded without hesitation, "Our God is with us, and he will not suffer that we should fall; [so] let us go forth." They believed that "if they did not doubt, God would deliver them" (Alma 56:46–47).

Not only was their faith in the Lord strong at the beginning of their march, but it remained strong throughout their ordeal. Every one of these young men was wounded, and at one point they nearly starved to death (see Alma 57:25; 58:7). Yet instead of wavering, they turned to the Lord and pled for strength—which they received (see Alma 58:10–12). Having faith didn't make their challenges disappear. It didn't make marching in Helaman's army easy. It didn't disqualify them from pain. But their faith did enable them to draw upon the power of God. Consequently, they "fought as if with the strength of God; yea, never were men known to have fought with such miraculous strength; and with such mighty power" (Alma 56:56).

We will not win the battle in which we are engaged if we do not fight as with the strength of God, for the voices of Satan are noisy, relentless, and celebrated. The gap between the way men and women of God and the way men and women of the world live will only grow wider. But that's okay, as long as we, the Lord's covenant people, feel confident about who we are.

We have every reason to, for when Nephi foresaw the latter-day Church, he "beheld the power of the Lamb of God, that it descended upon the saints of the church of the Lamb, and upon the covenant people of the Lord, who were scattered upon all the face of the earth; and they were armed with righteousness and with the power of God in great glory" (1 Nephi 14:14).

Nephi was seeing you and me. We may be small numerically, but the influence of those armed with righteousness and the power of God in great glory will be felt far beyond our numbers. We can't win this battle alone, but we aren't required to, for it is in the strength of the Lord that we can do all things (see Alma 26:12). And that process begins with our faith.

4. *The stripling warriors' faith began at home.* "They had been taught by their mothers, that if they did not doubt, God would deliver them" (Alma 56:47). Not only did those righteous, faithful, dedicated mothers teach their sons the gospel, but the stripling warriors listened, which almost certainly prepared them to follow the prophet Helaman into battle when the time came for them to do so. The lesson for us is clear: Choose carefully whom you listen to, and then listen. Choose carefully whom you will follow, and then follow. Listen to righteous parents and leaders, and certainly to prophets, seers, and revelators whose counsel is motivated only by their desire to teach truth and by their belief in our divine potential.

Satan tries to confuse us about voices and heroes and role models. He encourages us to worship the bright and beautiful—regardless of their values or motives. He makes the lives of the rich and famous look intoxicating when in reality many are just intoxicated. Just because someone can shoot a ball through a hoop or record a hit song or launch a billion-dollar IPO doesn't mean that he or she deserves our respect, and it *certainly* doesn't mean their lives should be patterns for our lives. Jesus Christ gave us the one sure pattern. If we are wise, we will follow only those who lead us closer to Him. That is the litmus test for evaluating anyone's motives.

5. *Happiness and lasting joy come only from living the gospel.* Said Helaman after leading his two thousand into battle, "I was filled with exceeding joy because of the goodness of God in preserving us" (Alma 57:36). Joy and righteousness are inseparably connected—though Satan would have us believe just the opposite, that joy and worldly pleasures are one and the same. But they are not. Likewise, Satan would have us believe that happiness cannot be found in obedience, which he portrays as confining rather than liberating. But that, of course, is a lie.

Here is just one example. In today's world, where immorality is celebrated on nearly every world stage, succumbing to moral temptation is depicted as being easier and even more desirable and enlightened than maintaining moral purity. But it isn't. The moment of sexual transgression is the last moment immorality is easy. I have never known anyone who was happier or who felt better about themselves or who had greater peace of mind as a result of their immorality. Never.

As someone who has remained unmarried two and a half decades beyond a traditional marriageable age, I know something about the challenge of chastity. It is not always easy, but it is far easier than regret or the loss of self-respect, than the agony of breaking covenants, than struggling with shallow and failed relationships. This is not to say there are never temptations. Even in my late forties, having long ago decided how I wanted to live my life, I have to be careful all the time. Morality isn't automatic; it requires constant awareness and effort. There are things I simply cannot watch, cannot read, cannot listen to because they trigger thoughts and instincts that drive the Spirit away and that edge me too close to the moral line. But those supposed sacrifices are well worth it.

It is so much more comforting to live with the Spirit than without, so much more joyful to have relationships of trust and true friendship than to indulge in a physical relationship that would eventually crumble anyway. Whereas Satan's lies lead only to enslavement, the Savior's promise is one of exaltation and endless lives. In other words, we shall have joy in this life and a fulness in the life hereafter. Righteousness begets happiness.

There are many other lessons we could learn from the sons of Helaman. We could talk of service and selflessness, of obedience and consecration and endurance. But I turn now to the final and perhaps most compelling point.

6. *It was the rising generation who bolstered and strengthened the body of the Church and who stepped forward to save the day.* When their help was needed, the stripling warriors were ready, worthy, and willing to respond. Again and again they came to the rescue, often reinforcing the older Nephite army who wore down as the battle wore on. The stripling warriors were like the cavalry in those old Westerns who arrived in the nick of time to save the day.

As with Helaman's young army, our young adult men and women are the cavalry, here to carry on the work of the Lord at an intense and vital stage of the battle—a battle that began with the war in heaven and that rages to this very day. Helaman told Moroni that his "little force" had given the Nephite army "great hopes and much joy" (Alma 56:17). As compared with Helaman's two thousand, today there are nearly two million young men and women in this Church between the ages of eighteen and twenty-five. Nevertheless, compared with the world's population and its escalating depravity, they are a "little force." But also, as in Helaman's day, we of older generations must rejoice in their strength and in their goodness. They bring great hope and much joy to the body of the Church. They are latter-day reinforcements prepared during aeons of premortality to face the enemy, reinforcements who must now step up to strengthen the body of the Church and help us keep moving steadily forward. And it is the responsibility of all of us—their parents and grandparents, aunts and uncles, teachers and friends—to help raise and lead this chosen generation.

Relief Society assignments have taken me to many countries where I have witnessed a remarkable trend. In countries such as Cambodia, Indonesia, Ghana, and Kenya, where the Church is young but the Spirit is strong, it is young men and women who are recognizing the truth, joining the Church, and being called upon to lead. The district Relief Society and Young Women presidents in Phnom Penh are each scarcely twenty years old. And I will never forget a Cambodia district conference when thirty handsome young Cambodian men stood and sang, "We are as the army of Helaman. We have been taught in our youth" (*Children's Songbook*, 172–73). They *are* the future of the Church in Cambodia. They will help save the day in their corner of the world—as will every one of our youth who lives on the Lord's side of the line.

After President Hinckley's appearance on *60 Minutes*, a non-LDS viewer sent this note to CBS: "I enjoyed your Mormon segment Easter Sunday. . . . These people do provide an anchor in a sea of ever-changing values. Fifty thousand chaste missionaries in 150 countries probably do more good for society than all the government social programs put together" (Tom Thorkelson to *60 Minutes*, 8 April 1996). Imagine then what an army of two million chaste, honest, dedicated young men and women filled with the power of God in great glory can do—and must do! There is no greater cause. There is no greater army for righteousness.

The Lord needs faithful, articulate, committed men and women, and young men and young women, who are undaunted by what lies ahead and who are willing to stand up for what is right again and again; who do not doubt what the Lord will do for them; who keep their covenants with exactness; and who have decided that, at all costs, they will live on the Lord's side of the line.

Will you commit to be true to who you are? To plant your feet in tar on the Lord's side of the line? I invite you to begin by taking inventory. There may be clothes or videos or books or magazines or CDs you need to throw out. Just do it. Toss out those movies that contain foul language and violence and sexual innuendo. If you can't resist adult Internet sites, unhook the Internet. No video or CD or Web site is worth crossing over into Satan's territory. No enticement is worth losing your exaltation. You will love how this kind of spiritual spring cleaning feels.

But that is just part one, the easy part. Part two involves taking an inventory of your language, your integrity, your dedication, your virtue, and the way you treat others. One by one, will you begin to throw out thoughts and behaviors and habits that pull you toward enemy territory? I'll take the challenge. Will you? The Lord will help us with this exercise, for if we will humble ourselves before Him and really believe in Him, He will bless us with strength we have never had before. He will help us turn our weakness into strength (see Ether 12:27). And every small victory over the natural man will be a victory over Satan and yet more evidence of the grand, sweeping, redemptive power of Jesus Christ. Let's begin now.

Make no mistake about it, the restored gospel *will* cover this earth. The battle will be rigorous, but the Lord will not concede and His kingdom will not fail. His power and glory will exceed anything we have ever seen in terms of dramatic finishes. For each of us, then, only this question remains: Will we stand steadfast and immovable on the Lord's side of the line? The Lord will be on our side if we will stay on His.

Every one of us has been prepared to stand where we stand in the kingdom of God, and we will be triumphant if we stand in holy places—on the Lord's side of the line—and be not moved.

CHAPTER 12

LETTING THE WORLD GO

WE ARE NOT WOMEN OF THE WORLD, WE ARE WOMEN
OF GOD—WHICH MEANS THAT WE NO LONGER HAVE
THE LUXURY OF SPENDING OUR ENERGY ON ANYTHING
THAT DOESN'T LEAD US AND OUR FAMILIES TO CHRIST.

I WILL NEVER FORGET a professional assignment that required me to travel to Jerusalem. I had been to Israel only once previously, and was eager to return. But I felt such a foreboding about the trip that I seriously considered canceling. Before doing so, however, I sought a priesthood blessing.

In that blessing I was warned that the adversary would attempt to thwart my mission, and that physical and spiritual danger lay ahead. I was also counseled that this was not to be a sightseeing or shopping trip, but that if I would focus on my assignments and seek the direction of the Spirit, I would return safely home.

The warning was sobering. But as I proceeded, pleading for direction and protection each step of the way, I realized that my experience wasn't all that unusual. Might not our Father have said to you and to me as we left His presence, "The adversary will attempt to thwart your mission, and you will face spiritual and physical danger. But if you will focus on your assignments, heed my voice, and refuse to reduce mortality to a sightseeing or shopping trip, you will return safely home."

The adversary is delighted when we act like sightseers, meaning those who are hearers rather than doers of the word, or shoppers, meaning those preoccupied with the vain things of this world that suffocate our spirits. Satan baits us with perishable pleasures and preoccupations—our bank accounts, our wardrobes, even our waistlines—for he knows that where our treasure is, there will our hearts be also (see Matthew 6:21). Unfortunately, it is easy to let the blinding glare of the adversary's enticements distract us from the light of Christ. "For what is a man profited, if he shall gain the whole world, and lose his own soul?" (Matthew 16:26).

Prophets ancient and modern have admonished us to be in but not of the world, to forsake the world and turn our hearts to Jesus Christ, who promised, "In this world your joy is not full, but in me your joy is full" (D&C 101:36). And for good reason. For in this mortal sojourn, wrestling as we do with the natural man's cravings for the enticements of the world, it can be easy to find ourselves lured away from the light of Christ by the adversary's blinding glare. Satan brilliantly blurs the line between the eternal things of God and the temporary, superficial creations of man. As President Spencer W. Kimball taught: "If we insist on spending all our time and resources building up for ourselves a worldly kingdom, that is exactly what we will inherit" (*Ensign*, June 1976, 6).

How often are we so focused on pursuing the so-called good life that we lose sight of eternal life? It is the fatal spiritual equivalent of selling our birthright for a mess of pottage.

The Lord revealed the remedy for such spiritual disaster when He counseled Emma Smith to "lay aside the things of this world, and seek for the things of a better" (D&C 25:10). And Christ provided the ultimate pattern, declaring prior to Gethsemane, "I have overcome the world" (John 16:33). The only way we can overcome the world is by coming unto Christ. And coming unto Christ means walking away from the world.

It means placing Christ and Christ only at the center of our lives so that the vanities and philosophies of men lose their addictive appeal. The Prophet Joseph stated simply, "If you wish to go where God is, you must be like God, or possess the principles which God possesses, for if we are not drawing towards God in principle, we are going from Him and drawing towards the devil" (*Teachings*, 216). Satan *is* the god of Babylon, or the world, and although his temptations may seem enticing they are temporary, deceptive, and laden with inevitable sorrow. Christ is the God of Israel, and His atonement gives us power to overcome the world. "If you expect glory, intelligence, and endless lives," said President Joseph F. Smith, "*let the world go*" (*Deseret Weekly*, 5 May 1894, 608; emphasis added).

As sisters in Zion we can be obstacles to the adversary's conspiracy against families and virtue. No wonder he tempts us to settle for earthly pleasures rather than seek eternal glory. A forty-five-year-old mother of six admitted that when she stopped poring over magazines that plagued her with images of how her home and wardrobe should look, she began to feel more at peace. She said, "I may be chubby, gray, and wrinkled; but I am a chubby, gray, wrinkled daughter of God Who knows me and loves me."

Relief Society can help us turn away from the world, for its express purpose is to help sisters and their families come to Christ. We simply no longer have the luxury of spending our energy on anything that does not lead us and our families to Christ. In the days ahead, a casual commitment to Christ will not carry us through.

As a young girl I saw commitment in my grandmother, who helped Grandpa homestead our farm on the Kansas prairie. Somehow they outlasted the Dust Bowl, the Depression, and the tornadoes that terrorize the Great Plains. I've often wondered how Grandma put up with years of meager income and hard work, and how she went on when her oldest son died in his early thirties in a tragic accident. Grandma's life wasn't easy. But do you know what I remember most about her? Her total joy in the gospel. She was never happier than when she was talking to someone new about the gospel or teaching a Sunday School class or speaking extemporaneously in sacrament meeting or doing family history research. She *had* laid aside the things of this world to seek for the things of a better.

To the world, my grandma was ordinary. She never made a best-dressed or a best-anything list. She never graced the cover of *Time* magazine. But to me, she represents the unsung heroines of this century who lived up to their premortal promises and left a foundation of faith upon which we may build. Grandma wasn't perfect, but she was a woman of God. Now it is for you and for me to carry forward the banner into the next century. For we are not women of the world. We are women of God. And women of God will be among the greatest heroines of the twenty-first century.

This is not to diminish the lives of countless good women throughout the world. But we are unique. We are unique because we have made sacred covenants, because of our spiritual privileges, and because of the responsibilities attached to both. We understand where we stand in the Great Plan of Happiness. And we know that God is our Father and that His Son is our unfailing Advocate.

At times the demands of our discipleship are heavy, for "of him unto whom much is given much is required" (D&C 82:3). But shouldn't we expect the journey towards eternal glory to stretch us?

We sometimes rationalize our preoccupation with this world and our casual attempts to grow spiritually by trying to console each other with the notion that living the gospel shouldn't be all that hard or require all that much of us—this despite the Prophet Joseph's declaration that "a religion that does not require the sacrifice of all things never has the power sufficient to produce the faith necessary unto life and salvation" (*Lectures on Faith*, 6:7). If we can't manage the relatively small requirements the Lord has asked of us, we'll never manage the larger questions—the largest of which is simply whether we have or have not truly chosen the Lord, as capsulized in Joshua's simple but profound declaration: "Choose you this day whom ye will serve; . . . but as for me and my house, we will serve the Lord" (Joshua 24:15).

The Lord's standard of behavior will always be more demanding than the world's. But then, the Lord's rewards are infinitely more glorious—including true joy, peace, and salvation, which is the "greatest of all the gifts of God" (D&C 6:13).

As Eliza R. Snow said, "[We] might as well have been born in some other . . . dispensation, unless *[we] can feel that [we] have a mission in Zion. . . . [We] are living to be Saints*" (*Woman's Exponent*, address given 14 August 1873, 63).

How then do we, as women of God, fill the full measure of our creation? The Lord "is a rewarder of them that diligently seek him" (Hebrews 11:6). We seek Him not only by studying and searching, by pleading and praying and watching always lest we enter into temptation, but by giving up worldly indulgences that straddle the line between God and mammon. Otherwise we risk being called but not chosen because our hearts are set so much upon the things of this world (see D&C 121:34–35). Consider the principle taught in the sequence of this scriptural injunction: "Thou shalt love the Lord thy God with all thy *heart*, with all thy might, mind, and strength" (D&C 59:5; emphasis added).

What the Lord requires first and foremost is our hearts. Said the Apostle Paul, "Set your affection on things above, not on things on the earth" (Colossians 3:2). Imagine how our choices would be affected if we loved the Savior above all else. How we would spend our time and money, or speak about each other, or dress on a hot summer day, or respond to the call to visit teach, or react to media that offends the Spirit?

Discipleship—and that is exactly what this process is—gives us cause to "rejoice evermore" (1 Thessalonians 5:16), for it is by letting the world go and coming unto Christ that we increasingly live as women of God. We were born for eternal glory. Just as faithful men were foreordained to hold the priesthood, we were foreordained to be women of God. President Gordon B. Hinckley has referred to the sisters of the Church as "the crowning glory" of the Lord's creation (*Ensign*, November 1995, 98). As the Relief Society Declaration proclaims, we *are* women of faith, virtue, vision, and charity who rejoice in motherhood, womanhood, and the sanctity of the family. We are not panicked about perfection, but we *are* working to become increasingly pure. And we know that in the strength of the Lord we can do all righteous things because we have immersed ourselves in His gospel.

I repeat, *we cannot be women of the world, for we are latter-day women of God.* As President Spencer W. Kimball explained, "No greater recognition can come to [us] in this world than to be known as [women] of God" (*Ensign*, November 1979, 102).

I will never forget my first experience on the Mount of Beatitudes overlooking the Sea of Galilee. As I sat on that storied place, I saw in the distance a city built on a hill. The visual image of a city that could not be hid was stunning, and as I pondered the symbolism I had an overwhelming impression that we as women of God are like that city. If we will leave behind the things of the world and come unto Christ so that the Spirit radiates through our lives and from our eyes, if we will cherish our covenants and "hold out faithful to the end" (D&C 6:13), our collective and individual uniqueness will be as a light unto the world. As sisters of Relief Society, we belong to the most significant community of women on this side of the veil. We *are* a spectacular city set on a hill. And the less we look and dress and act and talk like the women of the world, the more they will recognize something "different," even peculiar, in us, and over time, the more they will look to us as a wellspring of hope, peace, virtue, and joy.

More than twenty years ago President Kimball made a statement we have quoted ever since: "Much of the major growth that is coming to the Church in the last days . . . will happen . . . to the degree that the women of the Church are seen as distinct and different—in happy ways—from the women of the world" (*Ensign*, November 1979, 103–4). We can no longer be content to just quote President Kimball. We are the sisters who must and will make his prophecy a reality. But we can do it. I know we can.

We can begin by identifying at least one thing we can do to come out of the world and come closer to Christ. And then next month, another. And then another. Sisters, this is a call to arms, a call to action, a call to arise. A call to rely on the arm of the Lord rather than the arm of flesh. A call to "lift up the hands which hang down" (D&C 81:5). A call to bear righteous arms in the battle against the father of all lies and in defense of the Savior we have committed to serve and follow and emulate. A call to "arise and shine forth, that [our] light may be a standard for the nations" (D&C 115:5). A call to *live* as women of God so that we and our families may return safely home.

We have such cause to rejoice, for the gospel of Jesus Christ is the voice of gladness (see D&C 128:19)! It is because the Savior overcame the world that we may overcome. It is because He rose on the third day that we may arise as women of God. May we lay aside the things of this world and seek for the things of a better. May we this very hour commit to come out of the world and to never look back.

CHAPTER 13

STAND TALL AND
STAND TOGETHER

WE WHO ARE WOMEN AND YOUNG WOMEN OF GOD ARE
THE LORD'S SPECIAL TREASURES—NOT TO MENTION
HIS SECRET WEAPONS—AND WE HAVE A VITAL ROLE TO
PLAY IN HELPING BUILD HIS KINGDOM.

B Y THE TIME I TURNED TWELVE, I was a five-foot, ten-inch
social disaster. Towering over my friends was the bane of
my adolescence. I didn't want to stand out—at least not
that way—and so I compensated by slouching. As a result, Mother
was constantly urging me to "stand up straight." Well, I didn't
want to stand up straight then, but I do now. For we have all been
admonished to "stand up" (2 Nephi 8:17), to "stand with bright-
ness" before the Lord (2 Nephi 9:44), to "stand fast in the Lord"
(Philippians 4:1), to stand for truth and righteousness (see
Ephesians 6:14), and to stand as a witness (see Mosiah 18:9), so
that we may "stand blameless before God at the last day" (D&C
4:2). I can find absolutely no scriptural injunction to slouch in
Zion. Instead, we are repeatedly told to get on our feet, to "arise
and stand up" (3 Nephi 20:2).

As a teenager I did not realize or fully appreciate that blend-
ing in with the crowd would never be my lot. Nor is it the lot of

any woman of God who has made, and is striving to keep, sacred, holy, eternal covenants. The calling and expectation and responsibility of women of God is to stand tall precisely so that we *will* stand out from the rest of the world. Only in doing so may we hope to find joy. Finding joy and standing tall, not in feet or inches but as ambassadors for the Lord, are directly connected.

My family learned this truth in a most poignant way. I have seventeen nieces and nephews who are a pure delight. We have hiked and biked and fasted and prayed together. And we have also cried together. During the summer of 2000 we suffered a crushing loss when a fatal automobile accident took the lives of two of my sister Cindy's children—Amanda, who was eleven, and Tanner, who was fifteen. Because we have lived together in love, we have truly wept for the loss of them that died (see D&C 42:45).

Our friends in our small Kansas hometown, most of them nonmembers, wept with us, and with the outpouring of sympathy and concern that followed the deaths we realized that these people's hearts might never be more open to truth than on the day two caskets rested in our little hometown chapel. So we decided to dedicate the funeral entirely to testifying of Christ and the restored gospel. Afterward many told us how moved they were by what they heard and by what they felt. We were told that the common sentiment expressed in various groups around our little town was that they had never experienced anything quite like the funeral for Amanda and Tanner. Some even asked to learn more. It remains to be seen if anyone will join the Church as a result of our children's deaths. But this we know for sure—that standing up for what we believe and teaching the gospel to friends who had never before been willing to listen helped soothe our pain and bring us joy as a family.

In this world, the only true joy comes from the gospel—the joy that radiates from the Atonement and from ordinances that transcend the veil, and from the Comforter, Who salves our souls. I'll never forget receiving a letter from my niece Aubrey, then eleven years old, who had written her life history. Her words were unusually poignant because she had lost her father at the age of six and had had many subsequent changes in her life with which to deal. In her life story she told about a close friend, a nonmember, who had asked her why she didn't seem sad about the deaths of her father and her two cousins. Aubrey's reply was classic: "Not sad?" she said. "Trust me, we are sad. But we know that we will be together again, so we don't worry as much."

As a family, I imagine we have cried as much as any family does who loses loved ones. But there is no question that, because of what we know and what we believe, we don't worry as we would if we hadn't felt the transcendent reach and healing power of Jesus Christ. The gospel really is "beauty for ashes" (Isaiah 61:3), it is "the oil of gladness" (Hebrews 1:9), it is the "glad tidings" (D&C 76:40). It is such good news!

Though our children are gone for now, we have the glorious reassurance that we haven't lost them. But what about our Father's children, *our* brothers and sisters, who are lost and who thus face not only physical but spiritual death? The gospel of Jesus Christ is all about people. It is about leaving the ninety and nine and going into the wilderness after those who are lost. It is about mourning with those who mourn and bearing one another's burdens, with the ultimate burden anyone can bear being walking through life without gospel light—without a knowledge of who they are and who they have always been, without understanding why they are here having this mortal experience, and with no idea of where they may ultimately go.

Hence the Lord's latter-day plea, "The field is white already to harvest; and it is the eleventh hour, and the last time that I shall call laborers into my vineyard." He goes on to explain that though His vineyard has become corrupted "every whit," He will gather His elect from the four quarters of the earth, "even as many as will believe in [Him], and hearken unto [His] voice." As a result, He counsels us to "thrust in [our] sickles, and reap with all [our] might, mind, and strength," and then gives this glorious promise: "Open your mouths and they shall be filled" (D&C 33:3–4, 6–8).

Ancient prophets foresaw a day "when the knowledge of a Savior [would] spread throughout every nation, kindred, tongue, and people" (Mosiah 3:20). That day has come. And it is our turn to thrust in our sickles and help the Lord of the vineyard with the harvest. That we are here now is no accident. For aeons of time our Father watched us and knew He could trust us when so much would be at stake. For we are women of God, and the work of women of God *has always been* to help build the kingdom of God.

When in premortality we accepted our Father's plan, said Elder John A. Widtsoe, "we made a certain agreement with the Almighty. The Lord proposed a plan, conceived by him. We accepted it. Since the plan is intended for all men, we became parties to the salvation of every person under that plan. We agreed, right then and there, to be not only saviors for ourselves, but measurably saviors for the whole human family. We went into a partnership with the Lord. The working out of the plan became

. . . not merely the Father's work, and the Savior's work, but also our work" (*Utah Genealogical and Historical Magazine,* October 1934, 189). Then, when we were baptized here on this earth—choosing to follow the Lord a second time—we renewed our commitment to, and our covenant with, the Lord. No wonder President Gordon B. Hinckley has declared that "if the world is going to be saved, we have to do it. . . . No other people in the history of the world have . . . received a . . . more compelling mandate than we [have] . . . , and we'd better be getting at it" (*Church News,* 3 July 1999, 3).

We have our work cut out for us. The Prophet Joseph charged the Relief Society with the work of saving souls (see *History of the Church,* 5:25), for it is the very nature of women to nurture, to care about the well-being of others, and to search after those who are lost. And yet, more than a century after the Prophet's statement, President Spencer W. Kimball lamented that there was a power in the Relief Society (and therefore among the women of the Church) that had not "yet been fully exercised to strengthen the homes of Zion and build the Kingdom of God" (*Ensign,* March 1976, 4). For all the good it has done in the past, Relief Society has yet to help move this latter-day work forward as it must. Its members have yet to open their mouths and have them filled to the degree that the Lord is counting on. The time has come to unleash the power of righteous happiness that exists among women of God. The time has come for the women of the Church to be anxiously engaged in the work of teaching truth and saving souls. The time has come for the sisters of Relief Society to stand with and for the prophet in helping build the kingdom.

The time has come for each of us to stand tall, and then, in doing so, for us to stand together.

Standing tall begins with our own conversion, for when we taste the gospel's "exceeding joy" (Alma 36:24), we want to share it. The casseroles and quilts we have made to relieve suffering in more than 160 nations of the world are splendid acts of kindness. It would be impossible to quantify the impact that the 140,000-plus quilts made by the sisters of Relief Society during 1999 had not only on the Kosovar refugees for whom they were originally intended, but for countless others in need. It would be impossible to measure the cumulative impact of all of the acts of compassion and meals and home visits that 4.7 million women are offering every day of every year. The lives that have been touched and strengthened, the men and women and families who have felt the gift of kindness and true charity, cannot be numbered or measured—qualitatively or quantitatively. But absolutely no service compares with that of leading someone to Christ, of helping someone discover who they are, what they are here for, where they are headed—and how to get there.

Do you want to be happy? And I mean really happy? Then nurture someone along the path that leads to the temple and ultimately to Jesus Christ.

The most effective way to share the gospel is to live it. When we live like disciples of Christ should live, when we aren't just good but *happy* to be good, others will be drawn to us. We need to be happy about the way we've chosen to live, happy because we're not constantly reshaping ourselves in the world's image, happy because we have "the gift and the power of the Holy

Ghost" (1 Nephi 13:37), happy to stand tall so that we *will* stand out.

Every time we strengthen our own testimonies or help someone else strengthen theirs, we build the kingdom of God. Every time we choose honesty or stand up for decency, we displace evil and therefore build the kingdom of God. Every time we mentor a newly baptized sister or befriend a wandering soul without judging her or invite a nonmember family to home evening or give a Book of Mormon to a colleague or lead a family to the temple or exemplify modesty or celebrate motherhood or invite the missionaries into our homes or help someone discover the power of the Word, we build the kingdom of God. Imagine how it lifted my sister's spirits when she read this journal entry Tanner had made just days before he died: "Thanks, Mom and Dad, for teaching me about Christ." Is there anything that builds the kingdom more than does raising up a child to the Lord?

With the exception of those serving full-time missions, we need not don name badges or knock on doors to help build the kingdom. This process doesn't have to be scary; it doesn't need to be intimidating or overwhelming. For though some in the world would portray us as dowdy and dominated rather than the dynamic, radiant women we are, no woman is more persuasive, no woman has greater influence for good, no woman is a more vibrant instrument in the hands of the Lord than a woman of God who is thrilled to be who she is! I like to think of us as the Lord's secret weapon. For few people can resist a woman who lives and conducts her life under the influence of the Holy Ghost.

Imagine what would happen throughout this Church if every morning 4.7 million of us got on our knees and pleaded with our Father to know whom He needed us to reach out to that day. And then imagine if we followed those promptings! Imagine if we consecrated our energy and our focus en masse to the greatest service of all, that of leading our sisters and brothers to Christ. Imagine if we prayed every day for a missionary experience (which prayers are almost always answered, and quickly). Imagine what *will* happen when we mobilize the sisters of Relief Society as well as our spectacular young women, who President Hinckley has declared are part of the finest generation to ever come to earth and are thus among the finest women to have ever lived, to stand together to help build the kingdom. We will see the awakening and arising of a sleeping, slouching giant—the giant that President Kimball said had yet to reach its potential or maximize its mission.

President Gordon B. Hinckley has repeatedly invited us to rededicate our lives to building the kingdom. "I wish I could awaken in the heart of every man, woman, boy, and girl . . . the great consuming desire to share the gospel with others," he stated at a regional conference in Anchorage, Alaska. "If you do that you live better, you try to make your lives more exemplary because you know that those you teach will not believe unless you back up what you say by the goodness of your lives. Nobody can foretell the consequences of that which you do when you teach the gospel to another" (*Teachings of Gordon B. Hinckley,* 374).

The Lord has invited us, has pleaded with us, has admonished us to stand tall and to thrust in our sickle and join in this work, His work, with vigor. To reach out to someone who has wandered. To take new members under our wing and help them make the sometimes difficult transition into full-fledged fellowship in the Church. To consider serving missions with our husbands. To look and pray for missionary experiences and opportunities and moments. To make a difference in someone's life spiritually, especially the members of our own families. None of us have to reach everyone. But what if we all reached someone? And then someone else? And so on. President Hinckley has asked us "to become a vast army with enthusiasm for this work" (*Ensign,* May 1999, 110). As we do so, we will become one of the mightiest forces for good this world has ever seen. For we, the sisters of Relief Society, are women of God. And the work of women of God and the work of the Relief Society *has always been* to help build the kingdom of God. I believe that we can do more than we have ever done before to help our priesthood leaders with this great work, beginning with our prophet and continuing to include every bishop and branch president in the Church.

In my nephew's priesthood quorum, just a few hours before he died, Tanner said this: "You know, if I were to die soon, I would want my funeral to be a missionary farewell." Could we not be equally clear about our mission as women of God? We do not belong to just a really nice church that teaches really nice ideas so that we can live really nice lives. We belong to The Church of Jesus Christ of Latter-day Saints, which is endowed with His power and charged with carrying His truth to the ends of the earth. I love our Father. And I love His Son. This is Their work and Their glory, and we are the most blessed of all women to have such a vital part in it—a part that no one else can duplicate or replace.

We will find and experience joy as we lift our "voices as with the sound of a trump" (D&C 42:6), for as we stand tall and stand together we will see the work of God go forward boldly and nobly until "it has penetrated every continent, visited every clime, swept every country, and sounded in every ear, till the purposes of God shall be accomplished, and the Great Jehovah shall say the work is done" (*History of the Church*, 4:540).

CHAPTER 14

SHALL WE NOT GO FORWARD IN SO GREAT A CAUSE?

AS AN ANCIENT PROPHET FORETOLD, WE HAVE BEEN
ARMED WITH RIGHTEOUSNESS AND WITH THE POWER
OF GOD IN GREAT GLORY—AND THUS OUR INFLUENCE
WILL FAR EXCEED OUR NUMBERS.

N OT LONG AGO, we welcomed in a new millennium—
and not just any old millennium, but the era foreseen by
prophets from the beginning of time. What a magnificent time to take our turn in helping shoulder the glorious burden of the gospel kingdom!

I love the magnitude and the drama of it all. But then, I love
drum rolls and bugles and big finishes and anything that stirs our
souls and moves us to righteous action. This is just one reason I
am drawn to the Prophet Joseph's exuberant declaration: "Now,
what do we hear in the gospel which we have received? A voice of
gladness! . . . Shall we not go on in so great a cause? Go forward
and not backward. Courage, . . . and on, on to the victory!" (D&C
128:19, 22).

Doesn't that just make you want to climb a rooftop or go on
CNN and tell the whole world what you know and believe? We

are engaged in the glorious cause of Jesus Christ. Nonetheless, standing firm in that cause is not always easy to do.

When I was fifteen, I was invited to speak about the Church in my high school. Everyone knew I was LDS. Some of my friends had even come to Mutual with me. But as the only LDS girl in school, I often found myself trying to maintain that delicate balance between standing up for what I believed while not standing out. As the day of my presentation approached, I began to panic. How would my friends react to the story about Joseph Smith and angels and gold plates? I am sorry to admit that fear got the best of me, and I backed out. Afterward I was so ashamed. I had let the Lord down, and I knew it. But I had been more concerned about the praise of the in-crowd than the praise of the Lord. I had cared more about belonging to the "right" group than standing as a witness.

I imagine we have each had moments when we could and should have been more valiant in our testimonies of Jesus Christ, moments when in our desire to belong we turned our backs on the Master. We each have a longing to belong—to feel that we "fit in," to be part of something greater and grander than we are—so we scurry about, sometimes chasing worldly distinctions that give us the illusion of importance and acceptance. But ironically, as the Lord's covenant people, we already belong to an extraordinary "in-crowd," and we have the potential of belonging to the most exclusive group in time or eternity: the family of Christ. That depends, however, on our willingness to go forward in the glorious cause of Christ.

Each of us, regardless of (or perhaps because of) our personal circumstances, has a role to play in the latter-day kingdom of

God. Said President Joseph F. Smith: "He that sent His only-begotten Son into the world to accomplish the mission which He did, also sent . . . *every* man and woman in the world to accomplish a mission. . . . We [must] learn the obligation that we are under to God, and to each other, and . . . to the cause of Zion" (in Conference Report, October 1907, 3; emphasis added).

I acknowledge that not everyone is interested in focusing on the challenge of living up to our individual missions. After delivering a major satellite address in which I had touched on this subject, one sister wrote to say how she felt about what I had said: "I did not like Sheri Dew's remarks. She robbed life of all its joy and fun. . . . We need to be more casual about things. She sounded like a voice of doom. I was very disappointed. I did not like being told all I needed to be and do. I have struggled to not get overwhelmed by all the Church requires. Telling me the Lord expects valiant women did not help me. I don't want to be incredible. I want to be me."

I agonized over that letter, because the last thing I want to do is discourage anyone. But on the other hand, I dare not back away from what I taught that day or from what I wish to reaffirm here.

For there are three things about which I am absolutely certain: That Jesus is the Christ, that His gospel has been restored to the earth, and that every one of us has been foreordained to stand where we stand in the latter-day kingdom of God. We can't risk being casual about the Savior's work or about our role in it. No one else can fill my mission, and no one can fill yours. This knowledge shouldn't increase our burden; it should only reconfirm that we are beloved spirit daughters of God whose lives have meaning, purpose, and direction.

When Nephi saw our day in vision, he saw that those who would seek to bring forth Zion in these, the latter days, would be blessed, for we would have the "gift and the power of the Holy Ghost" (1 Nephi 13:37). Thus, during this culminating millennium, the influence of the righteous (that's you and me) will be far greater than our numbers or our natural ability—if we go forward in so great a cause.

It is on standing joyfully where we have been foreordained to stand, and going forward in so great a cause, that I wish to focus, drawing upon three principles from the Relief Society Declaration.

1. *As sisters, we are united in our devotion to Jesus Christ.*

I have come to believe that whatever we really want, we'll probably get. If we really want money and status, we'll find a way to get them. By the same token, if we really want to overcome bad habits or cultivate integrity or become more pure so that we can better hear the voice of the Spirit, we'll find a way to do those things as well. Fifty years from now, what we have become shouldn't surprise us, because we will have become what we have set our hearts upon. As Alma taught, the Lord "granteth unto men according to their desire" (Alma 29:4).

Satan is also after our hearts, because he knows that if he can control our feelings and desires, he can control us—which is why he tries to harden our hearts, puff up the pride of our hearts, and set our hearts upon the vain things of the world (see 4 Nephi 1:28; 2 Nephi 33:2; 28:15; Helaman 12:4). The Nephite civilization collapsed entirely once the people were past feeling (see Moroni

9:20). Likewise, we have been warned that in the last days "men's hearts shall fail them" (D&C 88:91), and the nightly news verifies this sad reality. Children killing children. "Spin doctors" celebrated for their articulate cunning rather than censored for breaches of integrity. Violence that knows no bounds.

No wonder we are commanded to "come unto the Lord with all [our hearts]" (Mormon 9:27). No wonder the Lord "requireth the heart and a willing mind" (D&C 64:34). Notice that He said nothing about how gorgeous or thin, educated or affluent, wealthy or influential we must be. He simply asks for our hearts and our will, because that's all we have to give Him. Everything else is already His.

Ultimately we will become what we give our hearts to, for we are shaped by what we desire and seek after. If we love the Lord such that our hearts are changed, His image will fill our countenances. But if we love the world more, we'll slowly take upon us those characteristics. As Truman G. Madsen has said, "At youth our face reveals genetics. At fifty, we have the face we deserve."

I'll never forget a visit I made to the Missionary Training Center when an instructor there said that the missionaries liked to refer to the MTC as a concentration camp but that he thought of it as a consecration camp. Life is the ultimate consecration camp, where we learn to turn our lives and our will over to the Lord. Only in giving all we have may we receive all our Father has.

In early 2000 a Relief Society assignment took me to Africa, and the images of our beautiful African sisters are still vivid in my heart and mind. Their countenances reflect the image of Christ.

When they pray, *they pray*. It's as though they reach right through the veil and talk to a trusted Friend. And despite severe temporal challenges, they are a happy lot. By the world's measure, they have little—except happiness. By contrast, many of us have everything—except happiness. Their optimism springs from a bedrock faith in Jesus Christ, to Whom they have given their hearts. I've found myself wondering who the Lord is most concerned about—those whose temporal challenges are extreme but whose hearts are fixed on Him, or those who have more things of this world but who haven't offered their whole souls unto Him (see Omni 1:26). Hunger may be a problem in Africa, but our sisters there aren't starving spiritually.

Several years ago, I had an unforgettable conversation with a friend who listened patiently while I whined about all the pressure I was under. Finally he said, "Sheri, you always take on more than you have time for. You must *want* to live this way." You should have heard my rebuttal. I *had* to work. I was a stake Relief Society president. And I was consumed by a huge project that was demanding every spare minute. He countered: "But you don't have to do any of those things. You must want to do them."

It was several days before I admitted to myself that he was right. But coming to the realization that I did indeed want to do everything I was doing was liberating, and it made the burden lift. By the same token, once we have turned our hearts over to the Lord and decided we *want* to be like Him and are willing to pay the requisite price, the process of following Him becomes one of joy rather than white-knuckled endurance.

This is crucial, because even as we turn our hearts to the Lord, we don't suddenly become perfect. We do have to endure to the end, and we'll all make mistakes and have lapses in judgment along the way. But when our hearts are changed, we have "no more disposition to do evil" (Mosiah 5:2), which means that we no longer want to make mistakes. And the Lord judges not only our works but our desires.

The question we might therefore want to ponder is simply this: What do we really want? And what are we willing to do to get it? When we were baptized, we said we wanted to come into the fold of God (see Mosiah 18:8). But do we really? Do we delight in being called His people, though that probably means looking and acting and talking and behaving and dressing differently from the rest of the world? If so, are we willing to yield our hearts to the Lord? Those who do will be born again as the sons and daughters of Christ (see Mosiah 5:7). The choice is ours. For what we really want, we'll ultimately get.

2. *We are women of charity.*

I once attended a fireside where a General Authority began by asking the question, "How can you tell if someone is converted to Jesus Christ?" We gave dozens of answers about service and commitment and obedience, none of which satisfied him. Finally he said that although our comments were all good, he believed that the one sure measure of a person's conversion was how he or she treated others.

I frankly expected something more profound, but his assertion so intrigued me that it drove me to the scriptures, where after much study I began to see how profound his message was: When we turn our hearts to the Lord, we instinctively open our hearts to others.

After the sons of Mosiah were converted, their thoughts

turned immediately to their people, for they "could not bear that any human soul should perish" (Mosiah 28:3). After Enos's all-night conversion, he "began to feel a desire for the welfare of [his] brethren . . . ; wherefore, [he] did pour out [his] whole soul unto God for them" (Enos 1:9). The Savior taught Peter, simply: "When thou art converted, strengthen thy brethren" (Luke 22:32).

Almost every major scriptural sermon focuses on the way we treat each other. In His Sermon on the Mount, the Savior taught us to turn the other cheek, to be reconciled to each other, and to love our enemies and pray for those who despitefully use us (see Matthew 5:39, 24, 44). King Benjamin admonished his people to serve each other and avoid contention (see Mosiah 2:17, 32), to administer to each other's spiritual and temporal relief (see Mosiah 4:26), and to impart of our substance to one another (see Mosiah 4:21). Alma the Elder spoke of mourning with those who mourn, bearing one another's burdens, and comforting those who stand in need of comfort (see Mosiah 18:8–9). Joseph Smith taught, "The nearer we get to our heavenly Father, the more we are disposed to look with compassion on perishing souls" (*History of the Church,* 5:24). He also said that "it is natural for females to have feelings of charity" (*History of the Church,* 4:605.)

Knowing this, Lucifer works hard at undermining our divine gift. All too often we fall into traps he has designed that estrange us from each other. He delights when we gossip and criticize and judge, when we stew over perceived offenses or measure ourselves against each other, or when we succumb to such envy that we even begrudge each other's successes. All of these spiritually debilitating behaviors wreak havoc in relationships. Let us not forget that Satan resents any righteous relationship—because he will never have even one. Thus his never-ending efforts to alienate us from one another.

A while ago a woman approached me after a fireside and asked, "Don't you feel guilty for choosing a career over marriage?" Her words hurt. But perhaps her comment would have been different if she had known my heart, or if she had known how much time I've spent fasting and pleading with the Lord in the temple, seeking to understand His will for me. Only He knows how painful this process has been. But He also knows how grateful I am for the process, because it has sealed my heart to Him.

How often have all of us made judgments that are equally unfair? Why can't we resist the urge to second-guess and evaluate each other? Why do we judge everything from the way we keep house to how many children we do or do not have? Sometimes I wonder if the final judgment will be a breeze compared with what we've put each other through here on earth! I've had so much feedback about various aspects of my appearance when I've spoken in a meeting broadcast via satellite that I've wondered if we ought to have a special answering machine for calls that come in: If you liked our hair, push one. If you didn't, push two. If you liked the color of our clothing, push three. If you would like to nominate colors for the next meeting, push four.

All of this just wears me out, because the Spirit cannot dwell in a home, a ward, or a relationship where there is criticism. Contention neutralizes us spiritually. When we fail to champion one another, we in essence betray each other.

I love a story James Bender included in his book *How to Talk Well.* Apparently there was a farmer who annually grew corn that won top honors at the state fair. One year in a newspaper interview the farmer admitted that he shared his seed corn with his neighbors.

"How can you afford to share your best seed corn with your neighbors when they will enter corn in the same competition as you?" the reporter asked.

"Why, Sir," the farmer responded, "don't you know that the wind picks up pollen from the ripening corn and swirls it from field to field? If my neighbors grow inferior corn, cross pollination from their fields to mine will steadily degrade the quality of my corn. So if I am to grow good corn, I must help my neighbors grow good corn."

It is the same with each of us. Those who wish to live worthy, consecrated lives must help those closest to them do the same. Those who wish to live well must help those with whom they live also strive to live well. Those who want to be happy and feel joy must help others find happiness, for the welfare of each of us is connected to the welfare of us all.

No wonder in the second meeting of the Relief Society, Emma Smith urged her sisters to "divest themselves of every jealousy and evil feeling toward each other" (Nauvoo Minutes, 24 March 1842). And in a later meeting, the Prophet Joseph said, "Sisters of the society, shall there be strife among you? I will not have it—you must repent and get the love of God. Away with self-righteousness" (Nauvoo Minutes, 9 June 1842).

It is simply not for us to judge each other. The Lord has reserved that right for Himself, because only He knows our hearts and understands the varying circumstances of our lives. Principles and covenants are the same for all of us. But the application of those principles will differ from person to person. What we can do is encourage each other to constantly seek the direction of the Holy Ghost to help us make decisions and then to bless us with the reassurance that our lives are on course. Only when the Lord is directing our lives can we expect to feel peace about our choices. And His approval is so much more vital than anyone else's.

Another kind of judging is more subtle but equally destructive. How often do we describe a sister with words like these: *She's a convert. She's been inactive. She's a Utah Mormon. She's single. She's a stay-at-home mom.*

When we label one another, we make judgments that divide us from each other and inevitably alienate us from the Lord. The Nephites learned this lesson the hard way. After the Savior appeared on this continent, those converted to the gospel lived in harmony for two hundred years. Because they loved God, they also loved each other. And though previously there had been Nephites and Lamanites and Ishmaelites, there were now no "-ites," as the scriptures tell us (4 Nephi 1:17). They were one. The result? There was not "a happier people among all the people who had been created by the hand of God" (4 Nephi 1:16). It wasn't until they again divided into classes that Satan began to win many hearts. The Nephites never recovered spiritually.

Can't we get rid of the "-ites" among us? Can't we avoid this "hardening of the categories"? We gain nothing by segregating ourselves based on superficial differences. What we have in common—particularly our commitment to the same glorious cause—is so much more significant than any distinctions in our individual lives. I think again of our sisters in Africa. The fact that my life is completely different from theirs didn't matter. When we left that last meeting in Ghana, I wept because I felt such a bond

Do Not LABEL — it Alienates everyone

with them. We are our sister's keeper. Heaven forbid that we would ever make even one sister feel left out. If there is anyplace in all the world where a woman should feel that she belongs, it is in this Church.

None of us needs one more person pointing out where we've fallen short. What we do need are each other's compassion, prayers, and support. What if we were to each decide that from this time forward we would make just one assumption about each other—that we are each doing the best we can? And what if we were to try a little harder to help each other? Imagine the cumulative effect, not to mention the effect on us spiritually. Followers of Christ who pray with all the energy of their hearts to be filled with His love, the pure love of Christ, will become like Him (see Moroni 7:48). As we are filled with this love, we no longer feel envy or think evil of others. That's because "charity never faileth" (Moroni 7:46).

Charity is demonstrated when we give someone the benefit of the doubt, or readily accept an apology, or refuse to pass along a juicy piece of gossip. Might we more often contemplate in prayer the grudges we need to put behind us, jealousies we should let go, and relationships we could improve by simply laying our pride aside?

President Gordon B. Hinckley said: "Do you want to be happy? Forget yourself and get lost in this great cause. Lend your efforts to helping people. . . . Work to lift and serve His sons and daughters. You will come to know a happiness that you have never known before. . . . Let's get the cankering, selfish attitude out of our lives . . . and stand a little taller . . . in the service of others" (Liverpool England Fireside, 31 August 1995).

Lucy Mack Smith's classic statement is that—a classic: "We must cherish one another, watch over one another, [and] comfort one another . . . that we may all sit down in heaven together" (Nauvoo Minutes, 24 March 1842). There isn't anything righteous we can't accomplish if we will stand together.

3. *We are a worldwide sisterhood and members of the most significant community of women on this side of the veil—the Relief Society of The Church of Jesus Christ of Latter-day Saints.*

When at age twenty-five I was called to serve as a ward Relief Society president, I wondered if my bishop was responding to inspiration or indigestion. I didn't fit the Relief Society profile, which I saw as older, married, bread-baking women. (Please, don't misunderstand. I *love* older, married, bread-baking women. Some are among my dearest personal friends. But it's a description that didn't seem to apply to me.) But now, after more than twenty years of Relief Society service on the ward, stake, and general levels, my view of our organization has changed dramatically.

The story of Relief Society is the story of prophets who have believed in the divine nature of women. It is the story of an organization destined to elevate women in their stature, their behavior, and their influence—both in quiet, one-on-one ways, and in contributions that affect communities, countries, and even continents. It is a classic story of using the simple to confound the mighty and strong, for the Relief Society is the only organization for women on the face of the earth founded by a prophet and undergirded by the priesthood of God.

President Joseph F. Smith stated that this organization was "divinely ordained of God to minister for the salvation of the souls of women and of men" *(Teachings of the Presidents of the Church,* 184).

I believe that we as sisters in Relief Society have a divine mandate to help save souls, to lead the women of the world, to strengthen the homes of Zion, and to build the kingdom of God. Shall we not go on in so great a cause?

During the first general conference held in the magnificent new Conference Center, the huge hall was filled to capacity and thousands were still unable to get tickets. I half-expected President Hinckley to step to the podium and say, "This just goes to show that if we build it, they will come." In like manner, if we rally our sisters to build the kind of sisterhood the Lord intends Relief Society to be, the women of the world will come. If we radiate the light of Jesus Christ because His Spirit shines in our eyes, because we tell the truth and teach our children to tell the truth, because we treat each other with gentleness, because we are modest but beautiful in the way we dress and speak and act, because we are quick to attribute benevolent intent to each other's actions, because we are armed with righteousness and with the power of God in great glory, and because we love Jesus Christ and are trying to follow Him—the good women of the world will look to us in increasing numbers and increasing ways. Our influence will be penetrating and persuasive. Make no mistake about it: We have been foreordained to lead the women of the world. To borrow a phrase commonly applied to the British Empire, the sun never sets on the work of Relief Society. Shall we not go on in so great a cause?

Some time ago I joined several other LDS women in hosting a group of wives of ambassadors to the United States. As we talked about the vital role of mothers and the family and the innate spirituality of women, several expressed curiosity about Relief Society. And when we exchanged good-byes, more than one ambassador's wife drew me aside and said, "There is such a wonderful feeling among your people. Could I find out more about your organization?"

If we build it, they *will* come. The Lord needs every one of us. He needs those leading our children and our young women. He needs every eighteen- and eighty-eight-year-old. Everyone who's been to college and everyone who hasn't. All who have borne children and all who delight in children. Lifelong members and those baptized yesterday. Those skilled at administering and those with a talent for ministering one-on-one. Those who speak Vietnamese and those who speak Portuguese. He needs sisters who can testify of the doctrines of the kingdom, sisters who can receive personal inspiration and teach with the Spirit, sisters who show by their actions that their hearts are centered on Him. He needs every one of us to fulfill our foreordained mission.

In the mid-1930s, Hitler began to make his play for power throughout the European continent. Winston Churchill saw through Hitler's rhetoric and began tromping up and down the British Isles sounding an alarm about this madman in Germany who was determined to control all of Europe. At the outset, Britishers accused Churchill of war-mongering and ignored his warnings. In those early days, it was unfashionable to oppose the charismatic German dictator. But the young Elder Gordon B. Hinckley, then serving as a missionary in London, found Churchill's petitions difficult to dismiss.

In June of 1935, at the conclusion of his mission, Elder

Hinckley and two other missionaries being released left London and set out for a brief tour of the European continent en route home. For several days they saw the sights by day and took overnight trains to their next destination. The trains in Germany were filled with Nazi troops, and Elder Hinckley was fascinated with their appearance and demeanor. They were spit and polish, their uniforms pressed and immaculate, their manner efficient and precise as they goose-stepped in unison and on command thrust their fists into the air in salute.

In Munich the threesome witnessed a company of Hitler Youth marching through the streets. "It was incredible to contemplate," Elder Hinckley said, "that a people would take fourteen- and fifteen-year-old boys, put them in battalions, and raise up a generation of soldiers. If I hadn't seen it with my own eyes, I would not have been able to fathom the insanity of it all."

In Dresden, as they visited a memorial to an earlier war, an elderly woman approached the monument. Poorly dressed, her face wrinkled with age, she laid a bouquet of flowers at the Unknown Soldier memorial and then knelt to pray. As she arose, her eyes filled with tears, Elder Hinckley could hear the sound of drums and marching youth filling the air. "History is going to repeat itself," he said to himself. "In a coming day, men and women will kneel at this monument and mourn the loss of the youths marching just a block away."

When he and his friends crossed into France, the contrast was dramatic. The French troops were not as disciplined or precise in their dress or their movements. Their demeanor suggested that they weren't as concerned about or prepared for what lay ahead. Elder Hinckley later reflected, "Hitler had identified his object and knew what he was doing. But the rest of Europe was asleep. I sensed that I had a front-row seat on the bleachers of history" (Dew, *Go Forward with Faith*, 80).

Similarly, *we* have front-row seats on the bleachers of an era in which Satan is moving about largely uncontrolled and unchecked. When Britain could have opposed Hitler and stopped him early on, the Britishers were busy doing other less significant things. They didn't recognize their enemy, and as a result they didn't prepare or marshal their energy and resources to defeat him. Other Allied countries were similarly nonchalant. And the results proved fatal for thousands of soldiers.

Today we face an enemy ever so much more threatening than Hitler, for what we have to lose is our happiness and peace of mind here, and eternal life in the world to come. Satan's tactics are bold and brilliant in both their subtlety and their impudence.

Satan knows exactly what he is doing. But do we? Are we sleeping, or are we creating places of security where we may insulate ourselves from his advances?

If there ever were a time when the Lord needed righteous, determined women who can distinguish between the adversary's deceptions and the voice of the Lord, it is now. If there were ever a time when the Lord needed women of integrity and purity who live in the world but rise above it, it is now. If there were ever a time when the Lord needed His daughters to be alert to what is happening in society and to defend the sanctity of the home and family, it is now. If there were ever a time when the Lord needed mothers and grandmothers, leaders and friends to safeguard their youth and children, it is now. If there ever were a time when the

Lord needed us to have a clear vision of who we are, where we are, and what is important, it is now.

It is therefore urgent that we covenant, and covenant now, to work and watch and fight and pray. To work to strengthen ourselves spiritually every week of every month of every year. To watch over and fortify our families and our Church family so that within the stakes of Zion will exist the strength and unity to help us withstand Lucifer's minions. To fight the adversary in every arena. And to pray with increasing strength and confidence and faith. The Lord has never expected more of faithful women than He does now. But we would not be here if we were not up to the challenge.

Historian Wallace Stegner concluded his foreword to *The Gathering of Zion: The Story of the Mormon Trail* with these words: "That I do not accept the faith that possessed [the Mormons] does not mean I doubt their . . . devotion and heroism. . . . Especially their women. Their women were incredible" (*The Gathering of Zion*, 13). Our sister forebears were incredible. And so are we, we who have come trailing clouds of glory, we who have foreordained missions that only *we* can fulfill.

Captain Moroni raised a title of liberty and invited all who would maintain it to "come forth in the strength of the Lord" (Alma 46:20). President Hinckley has done likewise: "We have work to do, . . . so very much of it. Let us roll up our sleeves and get at it, with a new commitment, putting our trust in the Lord. . . . We can do better than we have ever done before" (*Ensign*, May 1995, 88).

Among Mormon's last words to his son Moroni were these: "Let us labor diligently; for if we should cease to labor, we should be brought under condemnation; for we have a labor to perform whilst in this tabernacle of clay, that we may conquer the enemy of all righteousness, and rest our souls in the kingdom of God" (Moroni 9:6).

It is our faith and our works that will qualify us, through the Lord's mercy, for the exaltation of which Mormon wrote. May we labor diligently within our sphere of influence, large and small, to lead, guide, and persuade those we love and have stewardship for to come unto Christ, and to there partake of a goodness and sweetness that can be found nowhere else.

Shall we not, as women of God, go forward in so great a cause? Shall we not proclaim from the rooftops that the gospel is a gospel of gladness and that we are thrilled to be who we are?

I have reflected many times on the mistake I made in high school when I stumbled under the weight of popular opinion. But I won't do it again. I pledge to spend my life bearing witness of what I know to be true. Will you join with me? Can we stand together with our hearts devoted to the Lord and knit together in love one for another? If we will, the sisters of this Church will become a phenomenal force for good, a magnet and a beacon for those seeking truth, a haven for protecting the family and the nobility of womanhood. If we build a sisterhood filled with light, the women of the world will come. And we will become one of the greatest missionary forces this Church has ever seen. I repeat: The cause of women of God is to help build the kingdom of God. This is something we cannot be casual about. It is our steward-ship, our privilege, our destiny.

Jesus Christ came to earth in the Meridian of Time and did what He promised premortally He would do. Just as He came then, He will come again. And although He did not come in glory when He first came to earth, when He comes again, things will be different. For He will reign as Lord of lords and King of kings. The restored gospel will cover the earth. The Lord's kingdom will not fail. This means that for you and me there is just this question: Will we go forward in so great a cause? I declare with the Apostle Paul what I wish I had said thirty years ago in high school, "For I am not ashamed of the gospel of Christ" (Romans 1:16). In a coming day, perhaps sooner than later, every knee will bow and every tongue confess that Jesus is the Christ.

Of this I am certain. About this I have no doubt.

BOOKS CITED

Bender, James. *How to Talk Well.* New York: McGraw-Hill, 1994.

Cannon, George Q. *Gospel Truth: Discourses and Writings of President George Q. Cannon.* Selected, arranged, and edited by Jerreld L. Newquist. Salt Lake City: Deseret Book Company, 1987.

————. "Freedom of the Saints." In Brian H. Stuy, ed., *Collected Discourses,* 5 vols. Burbank, Calif., and Woodland Hills, Ut.: B.H.S. Publishing, 1987–1992, volume 2.

Dew, Sheri L. *Ezra Taft Benson.* Salt Lake City: Deseret Book Company, 1987.

————. *Go Forward with Faith: The Biography of Gordon B. Hinckley.* Salt Lake City: Deseret Book Company, 1996.

Grant, Heber J. Grant. *Gospel Standards: Selections from the Sermons and Writings of Heber J. Grant.* Compiled by G. Homer Durham. Salt Lake City: Improvement Era, 1981.

Hafen, Bruce C. *The Broken Heart: Applying the Atonement to Life's Experiences.* Salt Lake City: Deseret Book Company, 1989.

Hinckley, Gordon B. *Standing for Something: Ten Neglected Virtues That Will Heal Our Hearts and Homes.* New York: Times Books, 2000.

————. *Teachings of Gordon B. Hinckley.* Salt Lake City: Deseret Book Company, 1997.

Holland, Jeffrey R., and Patricia T. Holland. "Considering Covenants: Women, Men, Perspective, Promises." In *To Rejoice As Women: Talks from the 1994 Women's Conference.* Edited by Susette Fletcher Green and Dawn Hall Anderson. Salt Lake City: Deseret Book Company, 1995.

Holland, Patricia T. *A Quiet Heart.* Salt Lake City: Deseret Book Company, 2000.

In Our Own Words: Extraordinary Speeches of the American Century. Edited by Robert Torricelli and Andrew Carroll. New York: Kodansha International, 1999.

Journal of Discourses, 26 vols. London: Latter-day Saints' Book Depot, 1854–1886.

Lewis, C. S. *Mere Christianity.* New York: Simon and Schuster, 1996.

————. *The Screwtape Letters.* Philadelphia: Fortress Press, 1980.

————. *The Weight of Glory and Other Addresses.* New York: Macmillan, n.d.

Kimball, Spencer W. *Faith Precedes the Miracle.* Salt Lake City: Deseret Book Company, 1972.

———. *The Miracle of Forgiveness.* Salt Lake City: Bookcraft, 1969.

Maxwell, Neal A. *Notwithstanding My Weakness.* Salt Lake City: Deseret Book Company, 1981.

McConkie, Bruce R. *The Mortal Messiah,* 4 vols. Salt Lake City: Deseret Book Company, 1979–1981.

———. *A New Witness for the Articles of Faith.* Salt Lake City: Deseret Book Company, 1985.

———. *Sermons and Writings of Bruce R. McConkie.* Salt Lake City: Bookcraft, 1998.

Pratt, Parley P. *Key to the Science of Theology.* Salt Lake City: Deseret Book Company, 1965.

Proctor, Scot Facer, and Maurine Jensen Proctor. *The Gathering: Mormon Pioneers on the Trail to Zion.* Salt Lake City: Deseret Book Company, 1996.

Smith, Joseph. *History of The Church of Jesus Christ of Latter-day Saints,* 7 vols. Salt Lake City: The Church of Jesus Christ of Latter-day Saints, 1932–1951.

———. *Teachings of the Prophet Joseph Smith.* Selected and arranged by Joseph Fielding Smith. Salt Lake City: Deseret Book Company, 1976.

Smith, Joseph F. *Gospel Doctrine: Selections from the Sermons and Writings of Joseph F. Smith.* Compiled by John A. Widtsoe. Salt Lake City: Deseret Book Company, 1939.

Spirit of America, The. Edited by William J. Bennett. New York: Simon and Schuster, 1997.

Stegner, Wallace. *The Gathering of Zion: The Story of the Mormon Trail.* Lincoln: University of Nebraska Press, 1992.

Talmage, James E. *Jesus the Christ: A Study of the Messiah and His Mission According to Holy Scriptures Both Ancient and Modern.* Salt Lake City: Deseret Book Company, 1983.

Taylor, John. *The Gospel Kingdom: Selections from the Writings and Discourses of John Taylor.* Selected, arranged, and edited, with an introduction by G. Homer Durham. Salt Lake City: Improvement Era, 1941.

Teachings of the Presidents of the Church: Joseph F. Smith. Salt Lake City: The Church of Jesus Christ of Latter-day Saints, 2000.

Treasure Chest: Memorable Words of Wisdom and Inspiration. Compiled by Brian Culhane. San Francisco: Harper, 1995.

Widtsoe, John A. *Priesthood and Church Government.* Salt Lake City: Deseret Book Company, 1939.

Young, Brigham. *Discourses of Brigham Young.* Selected and arranged by John A. Widtsoe. Salt Lake City: Deseret Book Company, 1954.

INDEX